BWD

Th

A p

Do

Please return this book on or before the date shown above. To renew go to www.essex.gov.uk/libraries, ring 0845 603 7628 or go to any Essex library.

DS12 4005

Essex County Council

Samuel French — London
New York - Toronto - Holl~~~~~~~~

© 1981 BY DON TAYLOR

Rights of Performance by Amateurs are controlled by Samuel French Ltd, 52 Fitzroy Street, London W1T 5JR, and they, or their authorized agents, issue licences to amateurs on payment of a fee. **It is an infringement of the Copyright to give any performance or public reading of the play before the fee has been paid and the licence issued.**

The Royalty Fee indicated below is subject to contract and subject to variation at the sole discretion of Samuel French Ltd.

> Basic fee for each and every
> performance by amateurs   Code M
> in the British Isles

The Professional Rights in this play are controlled by Casarotto Ramsay Ltd, Waverley House, 7 – 12 Noel Street, London, W1F 8GQ.

The publication of this play does not imply that it is necessarily available for performance by amateurs or professionals, either in the British Isles or Overseas. Amateurs and professionals considering a production are strongly advised in their own interests to apply to the appropriate agents for written consent before starting rehearsals or booking a theatre or hall.

ISBN 0 573 11120 0

Please see page vi for further copyright information

CHARACTERS

Dan

Edmund

Margaret

Rachel

The action takes place in the living/dining-room of Edmund and Rachel's cottage

ACT I Afternoon

ACT II A short while later

Time—the present

AUTHOR'S NOTE

The Exorcism was written in 1971, at a time of great affluence in England, and when famine was raging in Biafra and Bangladesh. The play must be produced as a ghost story, but with the horrific realities that underlie it and were its starting point borne always in mind.

The first professional performance of this definitive text took place in Krakow, in a Polish translation in May 1976, and the first English performance at the Arts Theatre Belfast in 1979.

To my wife, Ellen Dryden, with love and thanks

COPYRIGHT INFORMATION

(See also page ii)

ACT I

The living/dining-room of Edmund and Rachel's cottage. Afternoon, Christmas Day

The play begins in darkness. There is a faint suggestion of harpsichord music, distant, only just audible. The Lights come up slowly, and we see the interior of a small seventeenth-century cottage, set in the English countryside, East Anglia, Hampshire, or Wiltshire perhaps. The first thing that becomes clear is that the building has been most beautifully renovated and converted, with an almost ideal combination of money and good taste. It contains every modern convenience and aesthetic refinement, but its essential nature has not been changed. It is convenient and comfortable, but still quite clearly a small labourer's cottage, not Hampstead transported to the countryside

We see the whole ground floor of the cottage, which has been divided into two quite distinct areas. The smaller is the dining-area, which at the moment contains a table completely set for Christmas dinner for four, lacking only the food. The rest of the ground floor contains the main living-area, and its point of focus is a large inglenook fireplace. The living-area is furnished with a comfortable sofa and armchairs, occasional tables, a drinks table and wall units filled with books, records, stereo equipment, built-in TV set etc. There is also an asymmetrical corner which has been completely devoted to music, with a large number of scores neatly in shelves, and with a small harpsichord as its central feature. Tasteful watercolours and prints decorate the walls, together with one or two carefully blended modern pictures, and there is a cunning arrangement of angled and free-standing spotlights and lamps to light the whole area. There is a beautifully decorated and illuminated Christmas tree, and the fire is lit, adding to the air of comfort and warmth. The main point about the set is its comparative smallness. This is a labourer's cottage, not a tenant farmer's farmhouse

Up stage, we can see through into the kitchen, which has clearly been built on to the main building. It is very brightly lit, and in keeping with the rest of the house, contains all the most practical and modern cookery equipment and labour-saving machinery, although most of this is not on view. Next to this is the front door. DL there is a small wooden door which opens on to the narrow staircase leading upstairs

As the play begins, the stairs door is open, and a low rumbling and creaking sound comes from above. Gradually we realize we are hearing footsteps from the upstairs room. The footsteps move to the staircase, and begin to come down the stairs

Dan enters the room from the stairs door, followed by Edmund. Dan is a large man, just knocking forty, carrying a little too much weight, and dressed in a slightly sober version of a modern safari-jacketed suit. Edmund is a smaller, dark-haired man, a year or so younger. But his hair is receding at the temples, and a customary preoccupied expression sometimes makes him look older than his age. He too is dressed in a suit, more conservatively than Dan, but still not too square.

Dan Of course, finding the right cottage is the most important thing.

Edmund Yes, we were very lucky.

Dan Did someone put you on to it?

Edmund No, we came across it purely by chance.

Dan How sickening!

Edmund We were out for a drive one Sunday afternoon, that's all. We parked the car in a lay-by on the main road—it's well over a mile from here you know, and with the trees you can't hear a sound . . .

Dan I know how far it is my dear fellow, your primitive trackway did wicked things to my suspension.

Edmund Well, we had to have that built you see, you couldn't get a car anywhere near the place.

Dan Well, you can tell your road-builder from me that it might do well for jeeps in Ghana or Mali or some such God-benighted hole, but for the home counties it leaves a lot to be desired. I advise him to emigrate.

Edmund Anyway, it was a beautiful evening, so we decided to go for a walk. We followed a footpath across the fields—about three-quarters of a mile over the back there—and then we saw the cottage, half-hidden in the trees. It looked so completely isolated—no other house in sight for miles—that we decided to go across and investigate. We'd always said that if we ever did manage to get a week-end cottage in the country, we'd make damn sure it really was in the country, surrounded by fields and trees and emptiness, not twenty yards from a main road. So we climbed a stile, crossed a ditch, scratched our legs to bits, and had a look.

Dan It's getting harder and harder. All the decent ones get snapped up in no time.

Edmund It wasn't much more than a ruin really. Doors and windows boarded up, and nettles three feet high, right up to the door. But we liked the area, it's reasonably convenient for London, and anyway, Rachel fell in love with it.

Margaret enters from the stairs door, followed by Rachel, who closes the door behind her. Margaret is a slightly scrawny blonde in her late thirties, with a quiet voice and an ironic turn of phrase. She wears a long and exotic dress, adorned with all kinds of ornaments, and several large rings on her fingers. Rachel is a dark and rather intense woman of thirty-five. She wears a simply cut dress in a sombre shade, which at the moment is protected by an apron. She still has about her something of the intensity and simplicity of the music student she once was, a certain quality of concealment all the more noticeable in the company of extroverts like Dan and Margaret

Margaret Rachel, it's lovely, really it is. I do envy you. Dan, I hope you're taking copious notes?

Dan I don't need to my darling, when it comes to excuses for spending money, you have a photographic memory.

Rachel It's funny about houses, isn't it. It's friendly here. You know how a house sort of welcomes or repels you as soon as you open the door.

Margaret We've been looking for years on and off. But Dan seems to think that beautifully decorated cottages just sit there in idyllic surroundings, waiting for him to take out his cheque book. Don't you, darling.

Rachel I felt it the very first time we came inside: almost as though something were saying: "You're welcome here."

Edmund (*to Margaret*) I was just telling Dan, the place was completely derelict. Been standing empty for years and years.

Dan Yes, well it's a bit off the beaten track, isn't it.

Edmund We had a hell of a job finding out who owned it. Took my solicitor the best part of six months, and then it was the land, not the building. As far as we can tell, the house itself doesn't seem to have any trace of an owner, even by descent. We drew a complete blank.

Dan Well, whoever owned it, farm labourers must have lived here. Family after family of them, right back into the eighteenth century.

Margaret Earlier than that.

Edmund That's what my father said. Ten generations of men who lived on bread and cheese. And now us. He sees it as symbolic.

Margaret Of what?

Edmund Oh, he didn't go into details.

Margaret No, they never do.

Dan And I suppose you got it for about fifty pounds, didn't you!

Edmund A bit more than that. Not too much more though.

Dan It's absolutely typical you know, these things never happen to me! If I'd bought it, it would have turned out to be a medieval pigsty built on a bog. I'd have ended up the owner of a very expensive fourteenth-century slum, not something out of *Homes and Gardens*.

Edmund I think you'd better have a drink. (*He goes to the drinks table*)

Dan (*following him*) I thought you were never going to ask. We've been here nearly twenty minutes . . .

Edmund pours Dan a drink

Margaret Did you have the kitchen built on?

Rachel There was a sort of shed thing. But we had to rebuild it almost completely and the loo and the bathroom, of course, that's all new.

Margaret Well, if you are going to live in the country, even at week-ends, you must provide for the creature comforts. I can't bear those dreadful people who lead civilized lives in offices and suburbs all week, and then go back to nature and live like cavemen at the week-end. They deposit their dung in piles under your bedroom window, because it's good for the soil, and when they give you a cup of tea, it's full of boiled newts.

Rachel Don't worry, we're very civilized here.

Edmund returns towards the two women. Dan follows with a drink in his hand

Edmund I should have asked you first Margaret, but Dan was desperate. What'll you have?

Margaret What have you got?

Dan Everything. They've got everything.

Margaret *Campari?*

Edmund With soda? (*He returns to the drinks table*)

Margaret Please.

Dan They've even got stereo in the bedroom!

Edmund (*to Rachel*) And you'll have a sherry?

Rachel Yes please, a small one.

Dan I hate to think how much it must have cost you.

Edmund So do I. (*He hands Rachel and Margaret their drinks*)

Rachel There was so much that had to be done you see, there didn't seem much point in half-measures. We thought we might as well get it as we wanted it straight away.

Edmund (*pouring himself a drink*) I'm mortgaged to a quite lunatic extent. But it's worth it, I think.

Dan Always spend other people's money in preference to your own, that's rule number one.

Edmund Well, of course. I couldn't have afforded it any other way.

Margaret The only thing we can possibly do in the circumstances Dan, is despise them for the shallowness of their bourgeois values.

Dan Quite right. When you can't afford something, moral superiority is the next best thing.

Rachel You're at the beginning of a very long story there Dan, so if I were you, I'd forget it.

Dan Oh, I'll drop it Rachel, it would depress me even more than it would Edmund, I'm sure.

Edmund I've got some photos somewhere, how it was just before the builders moved in. Where are they Rachel, can you remember?

Margaret Oh, spare us, Ed, please! I don't think we could bear it!

Rachel We'll find them after dinner.

Edmund (*looking through a drawer in the wall units*) It's all right, they're prints, not slides.

Dan That's the price of the meal, you see. A two-hour illustrated lecture, on the house, and how they made it so beautiful!

Rachel No, that I shall absolutely forbid!

Margaret I warn you, Christmas with Dan is usually ghastly. You don't know what you've let yourself in for.

Rachel Margaret, you're biased.

Margaret It's the same every year. He overeats like a pig at dinner, and fills himself up with gallons of red wine, then snores and groans his way through till Boxing Day. It's a memorable experience.

Dan Red wine! That reminds me! Margaret, where's the bag?

Margaret Oh, I think I put it down in the kitchen.

Dan Right.

Dan exits into the kitchen

Edmund What's up with Dan?

Margaret Oh it's nothing, Ed, he's brought a bottle of red wine, I do apologize.

Edmund Oh don't apologize. We've got a couple of bottles of Burgundy, but nothing very special.

Margaret Oh, with Dan it'll be *very* special, I can assure you! Dan is a wine bore. You'll get the whole decanting bit if you're not careful. (*Shouting*) Bring the bag with you, darling! . . . We've got a little present for you, if you don't mind.

Rachel Oh, well actually we've got one for you too.

Margaret Thank God for that! There's nothing quite like the frozen smiles you get when you give someone a present and they haven't got one for you.

Dan enters with a bag and a bottle of Burgundy

Dan Now that, my dears, is a truly magnificent bottle of Burgundy; as our little contribution to the celebration.

Edmund I know nothing at all about wine I'm afraid, Dan, it's wasted on me.

Dan Well, you can take my word for it, it's fantastic. I get it from a little place I know just near Covent Garden, the chap's a friend of mine, and he usually manages to . . .

Margaret All right darling, that'll do, it's a bottle of wine, that's all. We'll drink it and it'll taste nice and it'll probably put us to sleep.

Dan My wife is a barbarian. Where shall I put it?

Edmund It doesn't matter really. The temperature's more or less the same everywhere.

Dan puts the wine in the hearth

Rachel Where did you put the present, darling?

Edmund By the tree.

Rachel Oh yes, of course.

Rachel looks through the presents by the tree, while Margaret rummages in the bag

Edmund It's a grotesque business, Christmas, isn't it. It always strikes me, every year.

Dan If you're going to start talking about the commercialization of spiritual values Ed, I shall laugh out loud.

Edmund No, just the changes it's gone through. A primitive ritual, then a Christian sacrament. What is it now?

Rachel finds a small, flat parcel and hands it to Margaret

Dan The great festival of the belly, and none the worse for that.

Rachel There's still something in the present-giving, though, surely. As a mark of friendship?

Edmund Cases of champagne and bottles of scotch, for services rendered?

Rachel Not in business I don't mean. Among friends.

Edmund I suppose so.

Margaret begins to unwrap the parcel

Dan (*watching Margaret*) Now what's all this? It looks very exciting.

Rachel Anyway, Happy Christmas. I'm so glad you could come down.

Dan It was either that or enduring each other's company for forty-eight hours, so . . .

Margaret (*unwrapping a framed print*) Oh! It's lovely. Eighteenth-century, isn't it?

Edmund Yes. An original.

Margaret Yes, I can see. What's the house?

Rachel Well, that's the point. It's the local Hall. As it was in about seventeen-sixty.

Edmund It's not there at all now. Pulled down in the twenties.

Margaret Thank you very much, it's beautiful.

Rachel We saw it in a print shop in Charing Cross Road, and couldn't resist it. As a sort of memento.

Dan That's the life you see. All that elegance. I like the peacocks on the terrace.

Margaret And the ornamental lake.

Edmund Filled in, alas, probably with the debris from the house.

Dan I can't help feeling we've lost something, you know. Everybody ought to live like that. On second thoughts I suppose you two are having a pretty good try.

Edmund We lack the peacocks.

Dan Give it time.

Margaret My husband, you see, beneath his progressive, nay, radical exterior, is the most hardened reactionary. His ideal life style is the eighteenth-century *rentier*.

Dan Not at all. Nothing is too good for the people, that's my philosophy. Quite different.

Margaret (*giving Rachel a wrapped square box*) Anyway, this is our little offering. Happy Christmas, and thanks for the invitation.

Edmund What is it?

Unwrapping the box, Rachel brings out a small African carved figure, a woman giving birth to a child. It is ugly, distorted, both woman and emerging child have agonized expressions on their faces

Rachel (*a little taken aback*) Oh!

Margaret Sorry if it's a bit primitive and violent.

Edmund A woman giving birth.

Margaret A bit distorted. My friends who are mothers tell me it's not quite that bad.

Rachel No, no, it's beautiful!

Margaret Or indeed, ugly, but I know what you mean.

Dan It's genuine, you know, none of your Harrod's rubbish. Carved by a real live African out in the bush.

Edmund Where did you get it? (*He takes the carving from Rachel and examines it*)

Dan There's a shop just behind Knightsbridge, specializes in genuine tribal stuff.

Rachel They're ritual objects really, aren't they, these things?

Dan Well, fertility, I suppose, yes. Probably for rain.

Edmund But don't they make them specially for the tourists now?

Dan I'm sure they do, but not this one. This was carved by someone sitting in front of a hut after a day in the fields. Probably in a time of drought, or something like that.

Edmund It's a beautiful object though. Thanks a lot.

Margaret It's the psychology that fascinates me. You want something to happen to the weather, so you make an object which symbolizes your wishes. You use your imagination to create a fact.

Rachel All artists do that. When you imagine a thing, it becomes true.

Margaret Not only artists either.

Slight pause

Edmund Where shall I put it?

Rachel Oh, prominent on the shelf I should think. Clear a space. If you'll excuse me now, it's time I was seeing to the dinner, if we're ever to eat today . . .

Edmund places the carving on one of the shelves

Dan Good good! I'm starving.

Margaret I'll give you a hand.

Rachel Thanks.

Margaret Or at least, keep you company.

Rachel and Margaret exit into the kitchen

Dan What she really means is they'll have a good old gossip behind our backs. Got any dirt on you has she?

Edmund Not as far as I know. No more than usual.

Dan Nor me, as far as I know.

Pause

Edmund Is it worth it then, Dan? All this?

Dan Worth it? Of course it's worth it. Financially, once it's done, you can't lose. And who'd live any other way than in maximum comfort, if they had the chance?

Edmund Yes, I suppose so.

Dan But what I really want to know . . .

Edmund Yes?

Dan Is what does your old dad make of it all?

Edmund Well, yes. That's a bit of a sore point.

Dan I thought it might be. That's why I asked. Has he seen it? I gathered from what you said earlier . . .

Edmund Yes, we had him down for a week-end about a month ago. Rowed non-stop for forty-eight hours.

Dan On the lines you might expect?

Edmund Exactly on the lines you might expect.

Dan I can't help admiring your old man. I must do an article about him one of these days.

Edmund (*taking Dan's glass*) Do you want another sherry? (*He goes to the drinks table*)

Dan Yes please . . . It'd be nice, wouldn't it, if we could all keep our simple beliefs, regardless of the facts.

Edmund (*handing Dan his sherry*) Cheers.

Dan What did he say?

Edmund Asked me if I hadn't got anything better to do with my money— which is blood money anyway, as far as he's concerned. Advertising, public relations, market research, any of the selling professions, all out! Get over there with the goats!

Dan I should have been here and put the whole lot on tape. The working class and its wealthy sons! Worth a page or two in the *Statesman* any day of the week!

Edmund He fixed me with his branch meeting look, and said, "Eddie my son, it's no way for a Socialist to live."

Dan Did he indeed!

Edmund So I told him in that case I wasn't a Socialist. (*He drains his glass*)

Dan What did he say to that?

Edmund Nothing much. I think he was pretty shattered. (*Wryly*) So was I.

Dan The blackmail that goes on between parents and children!

Edmund And the other way round. (*He refills his glass*)

Dan After all, if one is forced to live in a bourgeois society, against one's will, as it were, I don't see why one shouldn't enjoy its legitimate rewards. I think we should be concentrating on how to be Socialists and rich!

Edmund No Dan, you can't escape the old man's logic. You can't think one way and live another. I've chosen to live like this, so I suppose the rest follows.

Dan Bad news for the Labour Party's millionaires.

Edmund Well, they live with their consciences, I live with mine. (*He smiles rather weakly and drinks his sherry*)

Margaret enters from the kitchen

Margaret Politics are forbidden at Christmas. Don't let him tempt you, Edmund. He's only collecting material for an article.

Dan I've already told him that.

Edmund *Campari* again?

Margaret Please . . .

Rachel enters from the kitchen

Edmund pours out Margaret's drink, and another sherry for Rachel

Edmund How long will it be, darling?
Rachel Not long. Time to finish the drinks.
Margaret Well, we're both green with envy.
Dan Shh, darling. Edmund's having an attack of guilt. They had a traumatic week-end with his father.
Rachel Oh, it wasn't that bad. They get into those two chairs and go at each other like hammer and tongs. They enjoy it.
Margaret The poor old boy's probably lonely. Likes nothing better than to come to his son's place for a good old row now and again.
Rachel Yes, I think that's right . . .

The two women smile, but Edmund nurses his own thoughts. The Lights begin to fade very slowly as dusk falls. Dan wanders over towards the harpsichord, and stands looking at it

Dan I can no longer contain my curiosity, Ed, about this beautiful machine in the corner. What is it, another affluent indulgence?
Rachel Oh, that's my Christmas present from Edmund . . .
Edmund Except that it arrived a bit too early.
Margaret Not new today then?
Rachel No, I've already been playing it for hours and hours. It's beautiful.
Dan I can see that, but what is it exactly?
Margaret Really, is there no end to my husband's ignorance! It's a harpsichord, darling, an early eighteenth-century piano!
Dan Oh yes, I know! Sounds like a drawer full of old spoons.
Rachel The way some people play it, it does, yes!
Edmund It is an indulgence really. But I love the sound. A piano seems out of place here.
Rachel I think it's a trick to lure me down here more often. He knows how much I adore baroque music.
Edmund And she does need something to keep in practice when we do come down, so . . .
Rachel Actually, of course, it requires a quite different technique from the piano, and the central heating doesn't do it much good, but still—
Edmund I'm afraid I'm not up with all the technicalities.
Rachel —it is a beautiful instrument.
Margaret Play us something.
Rachel What now? In the middle of getting the dinner?
Dan Why not? Something gentle and civilized, to usher in the feast!
Margaret You are pompous, how do I endure you?
Dan Play madam, play, ignore the interruption.
Rachel Well, let me see . . . (*She sits down, and almost without thinking she begins to play at once, a rather wistful and haunting minor key melody, with very simple and transparent figuration, in mid-eighteenth-century style*)
Margaret Oh, what a beautiful sound . . .
Edmund Just right for the cottage. Small-scale. Intense.
Margaret Lovely.

They all listen with genuine pleasure, moving to different parts of the room, to savour the sound, and leaving Rachel alone at the instrument, Rachel plays with all the concentration and musicality of a trained professional but suddenly she stops dead, in mid-phrase, and sits absolutely still, her hands still on the keyboard. Her tension immediately communicates itself to the others

Edmund What is it?

Rachel looks mystified, rather frightened. She remains absolutely still, and intensely abstracted, as though trying to remember something

Rachel This music . . . Something . . . In the back of my mind.
Edmund Darling . . . ?

Rachel stands up, and remains still, by the keyboard, as though listening

Rachel What was it? . . . That piece, do you know?
Edmund No.
Dan No.
Margaret Never heard it before.
Rachel No. Neither have I.

There is a silence. They look at one another, wondering what she means. Then she seems to recover herself a little

Sorry . . . I don't know where that came from at all . . . I can't think what it is, or why I played it . . . Funny.
Margaret Something lodged in your memory from years ago.
Rachel I suppose so.
Edmund You must have played hundreds of pieces like that. You could never remember them all.
Rachel Sorry to make such a fuss. For a moment I was quite frightened. I don't know why.
Edmund Frightened?

Pause

Dan *Déjà vu.*
Margaret What?
Dan *Déjà vu*, that's what it was: that strange feeling of having said or done something before; or when you recognize a place you're quite sure you've never been to. It happens to everyone. Like when a goose walks over your grave.
Margaret You can't beat him, can you. Always on hand with a superficial explanation.
Dan No, it's true. The wires get crossed in the mental computer, and it comes up with the wrong answer. Rachel's head, for instance, is full of music, but for a moment, her filing system's gone wrong.
Margaret Oh do shut up, dear man, or I shall begin to feel embarrassed!
Rachel Well . . . I'd better go and get the dinner out, if you'll excuse me. Pour some more drinks, darling, and put the lights on. It's almost dark.

Still troubled, Rachel exits into the kitchen

*There is a slight air of uncertainty between the other three. Edmund switches
on one or two lights and gets the sherry bottle to top up Dan's glass and his
own. Dan watches Rachel go, and follows her a few steps towards the
kitchen, then turns back to the others*

Dan (*smiling*) Hm . . . Hm . . .! Wasn't that interesting!

Edmund I don't know. Was it?

Dan Yes. Marvellous. Delightful! The slightest nudge of the irrational,
elbowing its way into our ordered lives!

Margaret You are a journalist, you know. You're a journalist from your
bootlaces to the centre of your tawdry little soul! Why the hell I go to
bed with you I can't imagine!

Dan Now what have I done to provoke such a brutal outburst!

Margaret The irrational indeed!

Dan What else do you call it? It was something that happened to Rachel
that she didn't understand.

Edmund She's not really like that at all usually. I mean, of course, she's a
passionate person. But she doesn't go in for—well, you know . . .

Dan Otherness! Not the world we live in, the world that lives in us!

Margaret That's all a load of mystic rubbish, Dan, and you know it! Just an
easy way out for people like you who can't be bothered to think things
through.

Dan All right then. Tell me. What really happened to Rachel then, at the
harpsichord?

Margaret She forgot the title of a piece of music.

Edmund (*quietly*) But why did it frighten her?

Dan That's right! . . . So let's be honest, we haven't a clue what went on in
Rachel's mind there, except that something did, and it caused fear. You
won't find anyone who can give you a convincing explanation of it.

Edmund But that doesn't mean it can't be explained, does it. Just that no-
one has explained it yet.

Margaret Don't deprive him of his thrilling little mystery, Ed, or he'll
have to fall back on his own intellect. And that will be a disaster!

Dan No, I'm sorry, my dears, but I won't be jeered into silence. There's
masses and masses of evidence by now, and it increases every year, that
the mind possesses other powers beyond the normal rational ones.

Edmund What powers do you mean?

Dan Oh, transference, survival, all kinds of things.

Margaret Show biz, darling, pure show biz.

Dan Not at all, there are countless authenticated stories: for instance, of
people being separated by thousands of miles being aware of the death
of someone close to them. If mind can be projected through space like
that, why not through time?

Margaret If.

Dan Haven't you ever stood on a battlefield and felt the presence of the
dead?

Margaret That's just imagination. You see a bleak field, and because you
happen to know a lot of men died there, you people it with ghosts. Your
mind colours the facts to suit its own preconceptions.

Edmund There's more to it than that, Margaret, isn't there. It's amply
proved, for instance, that the mind can have a positive physical effect.
I mean, hysterical paralysis, and things like that.

Margaret But your proving my point, not his! The whole point about
hysterical reactions is that they do have rational explanations. They
depend on cause and effect, not the supernatural!

Dan The point is, my sweetheart, that the reason alone can't be trusted,
that's all I'm saying. It can look at the facts, and because of its own
preconceptions, it can come up with the wrong answers.

Margaret That may be true, but it doesn't mean . . .

Dan In fact, it's particularly noticeable in your case, in spite of all this
arrogant pretence of rationality. I've never known anyone colour facts
to suit preconceptions quite as shamelessly as you do!

Margaret Why is it that with you, Dan, sensible discussion always ends up
with frivolous personal abuse.

Dan I lack intellectual fibre, that's all. Thank God for it too, or life would
be unliveable.

Margaret It's like being married to Coco the Clown. Ask him a sensible
question and he pours whitewash down your trousers.

Dan I have to steer her into the shallows of frivolity now and again, Ed,
or we would become permanently becalmed in a Sargasso Sea of fruitless
intellectual speculation!

Margaret Ugh!

Edmund Listen, do you remember that dreadful party game, Nelson's
Eye? It always frightened me to death.

Margaret No, I couldn't bear little girls' parties, hardly ever went to them.

Dan I remember it, but I wouldn't have thought it was your scene at all.
Very middle-class.

Edmund Oh well, we rough children were occasionally pulled in to make
up the numbers you know.

Margaret What was it all about?

Edmund Anyway, it was a great favourite at all the parties *I* was ever
invited to. I can't remember the details, just the traumatic bit.

Dan It's quite revolting.

Edmund You're blindfolded, and then you have to touch certain objects
and guess what they are. At the end they plunge your finger into a raw
egg, and tell you you're poking it into Nelson's blind eye.

Margaret Ugh!

Edmund It still makes me shiver when I think of it.

Dan It's a perfect example of what I was saying. And while we're on the
subject, I've just thought of an even better one. Sit still darling, and close
your eyes.

Margaret What? . . . Oh, what are you up to now?

Dan Are they closed?

Margaret Yes . . .

Dan No, I don't think I trust you. A blindfold will be better.

Dan takes off his silk neckscarf, and blindfolds her from behind

Margaret Oh ... What ... Dan! What's going on?
Dan That's better. Now stay there for a moment. (*He goes to the drinks table and begins to search among the bottles*)
Margaret What is he doing?
Edmund I don't know.
Margaret You know the trouble with Dan? He got to the age of thirty, and then started going backwards. God help me when he's fifteen!

Dan finds what he is looking for—the ice bucket. He picks up one cube and crosses back to Margaret, carrying it in his hand

Dan Eyes still closed?
Margaret Yes ...
Dan Right. Keep them closed. And Edmund, you say nothing. Just watch.
Margaret Dan, what *are* you doing ...?

Dan approaches her, holding the ice cube between thumb and finger. When his face is very close to hers, he speaks quietly and menacingly

Dan I have in my hand an open razor.
Margaret What?
Dan An old-fashioned cut-throat razor. It's very, very sharp.
Margaret Really, you'd never believe what some married people get up to.
Dan Quiet! Concentrate! I'm coming very close to you, and with this open razor I'm going to cut open your cheek.
Margaret Oh, are you. Charming.
Dan I'm getting closer. The razor's wide open. It's so sharp, I daren't even feel the edge. It would lay open my finger at the slightest touch.
Margaret My husband is quite mad!
Dan Still! Concentrate! Make the most of the last few seconds before the pain. I'm very close now. The blade is about two inches from your cheek. Can you feel how near it is?
Margaret Dan ... What is this?
Dan I told you. With this razor, I'm going to cut your cheek open ... There!

With a sudden movement, he draws the corner of the ice cube down her cheek. Margaret screams, and puts her hands to her face. Dan whips off the blindfold and shows her the ice cube

Dan An ice cube, melting. No damage done. (*He throws it on to the fire*)
Margaret My God, that did frighten me!
Dan Point proved, I think.
Margaret It was the coldness, and then the wetness on my cheek.
Dan You can kill a man with a drop of water on the back of his neck, if you tell him it's a guillotine.

Rachel enters from the kitchen

Rachel What was that noise?

Edmund Don't worry, darling. A little practical psychology from Dan.

Margaret My husband frightening the life out of me. Quite normal.

Dan (*kissing Rachel on the cheek*) Party games, darling, no need to get alarmed.

Rachel Well, dinner's ready now, so if you'd like to carry the turkey through, Ed, Margaret will help me with the vegetables and things. Oh, Dan, light the candles for me, would you?

Edmund exits into the kitchen, followed by Margaret and Rachel

Dan lights the two large candles set on the table, half-calling to the kitchen, half-talking to himself

Dan Oh yes, I'm all for that kind of thing, Rachel. There's a certain ritual about eating I should be very loath to lose. I admit, it's difficult to feel very close to the Great Spirit opening cans of luncheon meat and fruit salad in a kitchen full of washing up. But when it's turkey with all the trimmings, the candles are absolutely essential.

Edmund enters, carrying a very large turkey, just out of the oven, already set on a large carving dish. Rachel and Margaret follow him, carrying between them sprouts, potatoes, bread sauce, cranberry jelly, etc.

Edmund There we are then!

Dan Good God! That's not a turkey, it's an ostrich!

Margaret Isn't it a beauty?

Rachel Carve please, darling. Would you like to sit here, Margaret? And Dan, you here?

Edmund moves to the wall and switches on a spotlight, carefully angled to shine directly where he has placed the carving dish

Margaret Oh, you've gone much too far, Rachel, really you have.

Dan I warn you, I'm a terrible pig, I shan't leave any of this.

Margaret I've already made your excuses.

Edmund begins to carve as they all sit. Dan whispers exaggeratedly to Margaret

Dan My dear, have you noticed the carving light—neatly on the dish?

Edmund A little idea of the architect's.

Dan It's the little things that count you see, that's real style!

Edmund You're beginning to embarrass me.

Dan "You can't be a Socialist with a spotlight over your carving dish, lad!"

Dan laughs aloud, and they all join in as the holiday atmosphere and the presence of a beautifully cooked meal begins to take effect

Rachel No, really, we shouldn't laugh.

Margaret What's he doing for Christmas, the old man?

Rachel He's gone to Auntie Laura's.

Edmund We did ask him here, but . . .
Rachel The fact is, he'll be much better off there, he'll enjoy himself much
   more.
Dan Good God, I've forgotten the wine!
Margaret You talk too much, that's why.
Dan It won't have had any time to breathe!
Margaret We're going to drink it, darling, not strangle it.
Edmund Really Dan, I have a palate like sandpaper, it won't make any
   difference to me.
Dan This stuff's good any time, but we would have had just a little more
   flavour . . . (*He gets the wine from the hearth*)
Rachel Now, does everyone eat everything!
Margaret You can work on that principle, I think.
Dan Corkscrew?
Edmund On the table somewhere.
Rachel (*indicating the various dishes*) Well, here we are then, sprouts,
   potatoes, bread sauce, cranberry jelly.
Margaret Don't worry, darling, we'll manage.
Dan Now, let's see about this . . . (*He begins to insert the corkscrew*)
Margaret Suddenly I'm very hungry . . .
Rachel (*to Edmund, who is still carving*) How are you doing, darling?
Edmund Not too badly . . .

*Suddenly, quite without warning, all the electric lights in the house go out.
The stage is plunged into darkness, broken only by the light of the two
candles on the table, and the glow from the fire*

Dan Ah.
Edmund Oh no!
Margaret The bulb must have gone.
Rachel No, it's all of them. The kitchen as well!
Edmund Oh hell!
Dan How about that for timing?

A few giggles, mainly from Dan and Margaret

Edmund Must be a fuse. Sorry everyone.
Margaret Don't fret, dear man. No harm done. It's rather nice by candle-
   light.
Dan It's that little carving light you see. It's his special toy.
Edmund I won't be a minute.
Dan My dear fellow, we'll all wait for you. If it won't spoil?
Rachel It should survive a few minutes.
Dan And I shall save you the first glass of wine!

*Edmund exits into the kitchen, and after a few seconds we see the flashing
of a torchlight as he examines various appliances and looks at the fuse box.
As the others speak, we remain aware of what Edmund is doing in the
kitchen*

Rachel I'm so sorry about this.
Margaret Don't apologize, Rachel, please.

Rachel Just as we were about to eat.

Margaret The whole thing is so beautifully prepared, a few seconds' delay is only going to put a finer edge on our appetite.

Rachel Would you mind carving, Dan?

Dan Oh, well, if Ed wouldn't mind, er, spotlights and that!

Rachel No. Then we can begin as soon as he's changed the fuse.

Margaret You're not going to inflict the master carver act on us are you?

Dan Oh no, I don't have any fetishes of that kind. I don't care if they tear it off in lumps. (*He begins to carve*)

Margaret So I see.

Rachel Actually, the cottage looks rather nice candlelit, with just the fire.

Margaret It looks nice any old how, Rachel, when you live in the dump we live in.

Rachel I'm sorry to go on about it. It is rather a new toy yet, and we do love it so much.

Edmund enters from the kitchen, still carrying the torch. He is furious and swears under his breath

Edmund Oh Christ! (*During the following dialogue he walks about the living-area angrily trying switches, stereo, television, various lights, but nothing works*)

Dan We could never do it you know, Margaret, not even if we had the money. We have a talent for creating shambles and discomfort wherever we go. Every house we live in ends up looking like a bourgeois refugee camp.

Margaret Magazines, dirty underclothes and half-full cups of last week's coffee, it's all too horribly true.

Edmund tries the phone. That too seems to be dead, and he slams it down in exasperation

Rachel We had a candlelit evening here a week ago. I played to Ed for an hour, and then we read, and sat talking. It was lovely.

Margaret I bet.

Edmund Oh no, this is too much!

Edmund goes back into the dining-area, where Dan is still carving

Dan Don't worry, I've taken over, and I'm carving quite beautifully, even without the benefit of a specially angled spotlight.

Rachel Is everything all right?

Edmund No, it isn't.

Rachel What's wrong?

Edmund It looks like we've got a disaster on our hands.

Rachel A disaster?

Edmund That bloody electrician!

Rachel What is it darling, what's wrong?

Edmund Just about bloody everything! It's not the fuses, I've checked them, and they're all O.K. As far as I can see, we've lost all electric power throughout the house. No light, no heat, no cookers, central heating, television, the whole lot, kaput. Even the phone!

Rachel (*beginning to be rather upset*) Oh God . . .

Margaret No need to panic. You've all forgotten the obvious solution.

Dan And what's that?

Margaret This is England, remember? What always happens every year, as soon as it snows, or one or two people put their cookers and heaters on at once?

Dan A power cut!

Margaret Correct, a power cut! Either that, or the Government has decided to teach the unions a lesson. What better time to do it than at Christmas?

Rachel Oh, I do hope you're right.

Margaret Of course I'm right. There'll be a big inquest in the papers, and they'll all go on about how our democracy is at stake, and revolution is round the corner, and then forget about it three weeks later.

Edmund No, it can't be a power cut.

Rachel Why not?

Edmund The phone's gone too. That's nothing to do with the power.

A momentary silence

Margaret Oh well, don't worry, darling, it doesn't matter.

Rachel I haven't finished the pudding, or the coffee . . .

Margaret We've got enough food here to last a month.

Edmund You wait till I see that bloody electrician! Six months it's been done, that's all, and you can imagine how much it cost me!

Dan Well, it's probably something very simple, some little join or lead or something . . .

Margaret You will gather from that remark that my husband is no electrical genius,

Rachel (*becoming slightly hysterical*) Darling, if the heating's gone as well . . .

Margaret The fire will keep us warm, Rachel, don't panic.

Edmund I'm very sorry, I'm afraid this has spoiled everything.

Margaret Not at all. We've been dead lucky actually. The dinner's cooked to perfection; we just miss out on the pudding, and we can have that tomorrow, when we've got some appetite back.

Dan And there's gallons of wine and brandy and stuff, so we won't miss the coffee.

Edmund It's very kind of you to say so, but . . .

Margaret Let's forget all about minor inconveniences, and eat this fabulous meal.

Rachel I shall propose you as the perfect guests.

Margaret Well, we've all been hostesses in our time, haven't we.

Edmund I think I'll get some candles out.

Rachel Don't let your dinner spoil.

Edmund It won't take a minute. I'd rather get it done now, before we all start falling over each other.

Edmund exits into the kitchen with the torch

Dan I'll help you. Ladies, finish serving.

Dan follows Edmund into the kitchen

Margaret Any moment now I shall begin to get the giggles.
Rachel We'd planned it all to be so splendid. (*She begins to serve the food*)
Margaret The sight of Dan trying to be helpful is almost more than I can bear.
Rachel I suppose we could make coffee in a saucepan on the fire?
Margaret *I* wouldn't trust him with a candle. He'll burn the house down.

Dan and Edmund enter from the kitchen. They each carry two Victorian candlesticks with candles already set in them. Edmund lights them

Dan Society determines consciousness, Ed, that's what the Marxists say! But they've got it all wrong. Technology determines consciousness these days.
Edmund Same thing. Put your two over here.
Dan During the last batch of power cuts we spent whole evenings reading novels aloud to each other by oil lamp. Just like George Eliot and George Henry Lewes.

Dan and Edmund place their candles on convenient shelves, etc. Edmund stands by the fire

Rachel Do you know anyone who wants a beautiful cottage, all mod con, except that none of it works?
Margaret This is becoming a very moral tale. See how our civilization hangs by a thread! Throw a few switches, and we're back in the Dark Ages.

Dan moves across to Edmund, who is standing by the fire, abstracted in thought

Dan (*pointing to the candles*) Voilà!
Edmund Dan, I don't understand it.
Dan What's that?
Edmund If it were a power cut, the phone should be working. But it isn't. It's not conceivable that the phone and the electricity should have broken down simultaneously, surely?
Dan In England, at Christmas, anything is possible.
Edmund I don't understand what it could be that could affect both.
Dan Well, for instance, a large pylon could have fallen on a telegraph pole. You lack imagination, Edmund, that's your trouble. Now, let's eat.

Dan and Edmund return to the dining-area. The whole set is now candle- and fire-lit, dimly, but adequately. There are dark areas in corners, and the kitchen and stairs remain totally dark

Rachel Is everything all right, Ed?
Edmund (*quietly*) Well, you can see enough not to fall over the furniture now, at least.

Dan All right everybody, now let's forget all the little contretemps, shall we, and concentrate on enjoying ourselves?

Margaret I second that. Calm down, Rachel, all is well.

Rachel Sorry.

Dan It's very good for us anyway, all this. Gets us into practice.

Edmund What for?

Dan The great breakdown! When it comes.

Margaret This is the latest hobbyhorse.

Edmund What great breakdown?

Dan When all the machinery finally grinds to a halt, and we all go back to the land like our forefathers, and plough, and dig, and re-establish our spiritual kinship with the earth. All that sort of thing.

Rachel Sounds ghastly!

Dan Oh no, it'll be jolly good. The non-technological society! They'll still have journalists, of course.

Margaret Don't be taken in, Ed, it's all very simple. He heard a ten-minute radio programme on Ivan Illich, and now there's no stopping him.

Edmund Well, it hasn't happened yet. At least I hope not. So let's eat now, shall we.

Rachel At long last.

Margaret It smells delicious.

Dan All right then, we'll start the ball rolling with this bottle of wine ... (*He lifts up the opened bottle and smells the bouquet*) Mmmmm. Very, very nice. Try that for size, Edmund. (*He pours a large glass and gives it to Edmund*)

Edmund Well, cheers, everybody. (*He takes a large mouthful. Suddenly, he goes pale, grimaces, chokes, and spits the wine all over the table*)

Margaret Oh ...

Rachel Whatever ...?

Dan I say ...!

Edmund looks about to be sick, and spits and retches into his glass. The others are caught between mystification, amusement and horror

Rachel Oh darling, look what you've done to the table!

Dan Must have gone down the wrong hole.

Edmund (*still choking and shuddering*) No ... Ugh ...

Margaret What's the matter?

Edmund It's—not wine ...

Pause. They look at each other, not comprehending

Dan What do you mean, it's not wine, of course it is.

Edmund It's blood.

A silence of incomprehension and amazement, tinged with fear

Dan What?

Edmund It's blood. It is, it's blood.

Rachel (*quietly*) Don't be silly.

Edmund (*shouting*) It is, it's blood, taste it!

Silence, broken by Rachel's voice and movement

Rachel I'll get a cloth.

Rachel exits to the kitchen, trembling

Without a word, Dan pours a brimming glass of the wine, savours the bouquet, and drinks a long mouthful. The other two watch him

Dan (*quietly*) It's burgundy. Very good burgundy.

Edmund looks horrified, and Dan pours another long glass for Margaret

Taste it.

Margaret does so

Margaret Burgundy. Beautiful.

Rachel enters with a cloth and begins to wipe down the table and Edmund's suit

Edmund I don't understand.
Dan Taste mine. Really, I'm not joking. Here.
Edmund (*taking the glass and smelling it*) I must be going mad. It smells— just the same.
Dan Look. (*He drinks another mouthful*) Now, that's not blood, is it.
Edmund (*sipping it and shuddering*) Ugh . . . It is. To me it is. Salty, a bit sticky . . . I mean it!
Rachel Stop it, Ed, stop it!
Edmund What do you mean?
Rachel Whatever sort of game you're playing! Stop it!
Edmund Rachel, it isn't a game! To me it tastes like . . .
Rachel (*shouting*) It's wine, obviously it's wine, look! (*Pale and shattered, she takes Margaret's glass and drinks from it. Very quietly*) It's wine.

The tension between the four of them is completely unresolved. With a conscious effort, Dan breaks it

Dan Never mind, my dear fellow. I won't insult you by bringing my own wine next time.
Edmund I'm not joking you know, Dan. I believe you when you say it's wine. But to me . . . No. No. It isn't possible is it?

A long pause. No-one knows what to say

Margaret Let's eat our dinner. Quietly and privately, shall we? Wine or no wine. Before it finally gets cold.
Dan Yes. That's a good idea.

Dan and Margaret begin to eat in silence, throwing occasional glances at each other, and at the other two. Rachel, too, nervously addresses herself to her meal, and finally Edmund, who looks again at the liquid in his glass before taking a tentative mouthful of food. They eat in silence for some

*seconds, some taking mouthfuls of meat, others vegetable. Dan coughs
slightly, and swallows with an effort, then reaches to pour himself a glass of
iced water. Rachel's face drains as she chews her food, and swallows it with
some difficulty. Edmund watches, with a piece of meat on his fork, poised at
his lips. Margaret too begins to look strained, swallows, and reaches for the
water. Edmund looks at the meat, and deliberately puts a piece into his
mouth. They all continue to eat, but clearly with increasing difficulty, and the
beginnings of pain. They all look at each other, at their chewing mouths, and
foreheads beginning to sweat. Edmund reaches for the water, and Dan
surreptitiously puts his hand to his stomach. Rachel is verging on hysteria*

Rachel Oh God . . .

Dan (*in pain*) I'm sorry, darling. This is a very hot turkey . . .

Edmund It's the meat . . . It's the meat too.

Dan Madras style, and then some. Ouuuf! (*He groans and pushes back his
chair, still trying to laugh it off, but in some pain*)

Margaret Oh God, it's hot! Have you stuffed it with chillis and pepper
seeds? (*She grimaces with pain and holds her stomach*)

Dan gets up and moves away from the table, holding his stomach

Dan Don't worry, Margaret, I recognize a practical joke when I see one!
It's the big Christmas wheeze. Vintage blood, and a bird that tastes like—
acid! Owwww! (*He staggers and bends double, sinking on his knees with
the pain*)

Rachel There's no joke, Dan. It's just an ordinary turkey, I cooked it just
as usual.

Margaret half-falls off her chair, till she is on all fours

Margaret My God, I think you've poisoned us.

Edmund (*getting up*) What's happening? Rachel, Dan, what's happening
here?

Dan Oh God, it's burning me . . .!

Edmund Water . . . drink lots of water . . . (*He goes towards the drinks
table to get some more water, but groans and falls on his knees before he
gets there*)

Margaret is now almost flat out on the floor. She tries to rise to her knees

Margaret Oh God, this is agony. I think we're all going to die! (*She falls
back on to the floor*)

*At this point Margaret, Dan and Edmund are all more or less spread-eagled
on the floor in an attempt to lessen the pain. Rachel, who is clearly feeling
less pain than the others, is still sitting at the table, watching in horror. She
rises, slowly*

Rachel I can't bear it . . . I can't bear it any more . . .!

*Rachel runs across the room, seizes a candle, and exits quickly up the stairs
There is a long pause. Dan, Margaret and Edmund lie flat out on the floor.
Their groans begin to stop, and at the same time music is heard, so faintly as*

*to be only just audible, and not distinguishable. They raise themselves from
the floor, slowly, still in pain*

Dan Oh . . . It's going off . . . That's better.
Margaret Oh, yes . . . me too . . . Thank God for that.
Edmund Take deep breaths. That helps.

*The music now becomes just audible. It is the harpsichord music Rachel
played earlier*

Margaret Listen! . . . Can you hear music?
Edmund I can hear it.
Dan Yes, I can hear it too.

Edmund goes to the harpsichord

Edmund It can't be . . . Where is it coming from?
Dan Rachel, upstairs. She's turned the radio on.
Edmund There's no electricity.
Margaret Listen to it!

It is still only just audible, and never gets any louder

Dan What?
Margaret Don't you recognize it?
Dan No . . . Wait a minute . . .
Edmund It's the music Rachel played.
Margaret That's right . . . Where's it coming from? The air?
Dan Where did the pains come from?
Edmund Not from that bird, I'm sure.
Margaret With me it's almost completely gone. So suddenly. Just the
shadow of a pain now.
Edmund Yes. With me too.
Margaret It was very strong, biting and hollow. How I imagine taking
poison. Was it like that with you?

The music fades imperceptibly away

Dan Burning, terrible. As I swallowed the meat.
Edmund And now it's gone. Just like that.
Margaret So has the music. Listen.
Edmund Nothing at all.
Dan Silence . . .

*As they are all standing listening, Rachel appears slowly and silently in the
stairs doorway behind them, still holding her candle. She looks pale and
haggard, and for a moment says nothing, as though stunned*

Edmund (*suddenly seeing her*) Rachel . . .!
Rachel (*very quietly*) Did you hear it? Or am I going mad?
Margaret We heard music.
Dan And in answer to your second question, yes, we are going mad.
Edmund Rachel—are you all right?

Rachel puts the candle down, and walks slowly, almost wearily, to sit down on the sofa. She speaks blankly, almost without emotion, as though what she is saying is no surprise

Rachel Upstairs . . . on our bed . . . there is the skeleton of a child . . . I presume it's a child. It's only about three feet long, and the head bones are rather fragile.

A stunned, uncomprehending pause

Edmund What?
Rachel (*continuing in the same grey manner*) That's why I asked if you heard the music . . . Of course, you don't believe me . . . It's not just my eyes. I touched it too . . . There's a dead child lying on the bed.

Pause

Edmund (*quietly*) Come with me, Dan, will you?
Dan For confirmation, or support?
Edmund Both.

*Edmund and Dan take a candle apiece, and exit up the stairs together
There is a silence as the two women listen. Rachel is still sitting in the same position, and hasn't moved. Margaret crosses to sit near her*

Rachel You heard the music then?
Margaret Yes. We heard it.
Rachel I hoped it was in my head . . . Did you recognize it?
Margaret Yes.
Rachel Did it come from the instrument?
Margaret No. It didn't seem to come from anywhere. From the walls, almost. Quadrophony. (*She smiles weakly at her own joke*)

Rachel doesn't react at all, remaining still as before

Rachel That means it's something to do with me.
Margaret Why do you say that?
Rachel I know it is. The music came to me first. I played it before I knew it. I'm the one.
Margaret I don't see why. We all heard it.
Rachel I'm very frightened, Margaret. Are you?
Margaret I was frightened by the pain. I really thought it was poison and I was going to die. But I'm not frightened now. Interested really. Mystified.
Rachel I can feel something . . . I can't describe what it is. But it's something dreadful.

Pause. Margaret gets up, consciously breaking Rachel's mood

Margaret Well, I've always been a sceptic. I don't see any good reason to change yet.
Rachel You will.
Margaret When you think about it, it's a bit like a sideshow at a fair. All those cheap tricks and stunts catch your emotions easily enough. But if

you go round the back, and see the wires and pulleys that make them work, then they just make you laugh.

Rachel No, this isn't like that, believe me. It's terror. It's a black hole, beginning to open inside me. I can't control it.

Margaret Well. I don't feel at all like that, and it's no use pretending that I do. What has happened has happened, but I refuse to be bludgeoned by a series of stunts. Whatever it is, I'll be convinced when I understand it, and not before.

Dan and Edmund enter. They look at the two silent women. Dan closes the door

Edmund Rachel . . .?
Rachel Yes?
Edmund Rachel, there's nothing in the bedroom.

Pause

Rachel Nothing.
Edmund Nothing at all. Everything's just as usual.
Dan There's been nothing on the bedspread. It's quite smooth.
Edmund We even put our hands on it, to be sure.
Rachel My eyes saw it and my hands touched it. It still had some milk teeth, with the new ones growing underneath.

A long, unresolved silence. They all look at each other

Edmund (*deliberately flatly*) What's going on, Dan? Margaret?
Dan Something very strange. I feel quite all right now though.
Margaret So do I . . . but not hungry any more.
Dan No.
Edmund No trace of the pain?
Dan No, none.
Margaret No.
Dan What about Rachel? Did you feel it?
Rachel Yes, I felt it. A terrible griping pain in the stomach.
Margaret But it went quite suddenly.
Dan Yes, that happened to all of us. But none of us tasted blood, except Edmund.
Margaret No.
Rachel No.
Edmund I can hardly believe it myself.
Dan And then, this upstairs.
Rachel I definitely saw it. I didn't imagine it. I looked for quite a long time to make sure. And then I touched it, on the head. It was a child's skeleton, about three feet long, with bits of clothing, lying on the bedspread. I promise you, I really did see it!
Dan No-one has suggested you didn't. Equally though, we didn't see it.
Margaret But we've all felt or seen something, haven't we. Edmund the blood, the rest of us the food, the pain that just disappeared, and the music; and now Rachel, this.

Edmund And all of us the house.

Dan What do you mean?

Edmund We've all experienced that, the failure of all the machinery in the house.

Dan But that's perfectly straightforward, simple mechanics.

Edmund Is it?

Margaret What are you implying, that the whole thing, the power failure included, is some kind of mass hallucination?

Edmund Can you suggest anything better?

Dan In that case, we're still in the grip of it. The clocks are still dead, and so are the lights. If it's mass hysteria, something our four minds are creating between us, we're still under its spell.

Edmund Nothing's been right since the lights went out.

Rachel Before that. The music.

Margaret So what shall we do then? There must be some kind of rational explanation.

Rachel I don't need any explanation. I just want it to stop.

Dan If it is a form of mass hysteria . . .

Edmund How can it be, look, we're four sane and mature people, we know what we're saying and doing . . .

Margaret Do we though? We think all the lights have failed. But maybe they're on all the time, maybe they're blazing across the fields for miles. If you tasted blood, and Rachel saw a dead child on the bed, that's just as possible. Our perceptions tell us that we're sane and balanced, and that those are the facts. But perhaps that's the prime constituent of our hysteria.

Edmund So that we've lost all distinction, you mean, between what's really happening, and what's imagination?

Margaret How else can you explain what's happened in the last fifteen minutes? These delusions have come from somewhere. If not from our own minds, where? (*She gets up and walks restlessly over to one of the windows*)

Dan Listen, if what you say is true, then what we need to do, to re-assert reality, ordinary daily reality where wine is wine, and all the machines work, is to get out of here, and if necessary, separate: break whatever mental chain is binding the four of us together. So I suggest we go out, get into our cars, and drive away to some nice, crowded, uncomplicated hotel, where there's dancing, and an M.C., and they're all playing silly and innocent Christmas games. So that we dissipate whatever it is that's been deranging our perceptions here. Agreed?

Edmund Yes. I think that's a good idea.

Margaret (*looking through the window*) Dan?

Dan What?

Margaret The car was opposite this window, wasn't it? Quite close.

Dan Yes. Why?

Margaret I can't see it. I can't see any dark shapes where the hedges and trees are either, or even the grass under the window. I can't see anything at all.

Dan Let me see . . .

Margaret It's never absolutely dark, is it? There's no such thing as absolute darkness?

Edmund No, and anyway, there's light coming from this room, from the candles and the fire. It ought to reflect on the bonnet and the headlights.

Margaret There's nothing. It's like a black curtain.

Edmund moves swiftly to the front door and tries to open it. The handle won't turn

Edmund Dan, give me a hand.

They both exert all their wrist power on the door handle, but nothing happens

Dan Won't budge.

Edmund Shoulder it with me.

They both shoulder charge the door, with all their combined strength. Not one inch of movement. Not even a shudder. Margaret crosses to the window in the dining-area

It's not going to open, is it?

Dan No, it's not.

Margaret This window's the same. Like the bottom of the sea.

Rachel sits down

Rachel (*with a strange calmness*) We're caught in here, I know it. Something has got us trapped.

Edmund Dan, look at the upstairs' windows. I'll try the back door.

Dan O.K.

Dan runs upstairs to check the windows

Edmund exits hurriedly into the kitchen and rattles the backdoor with no more success than the front

Margaret sits by Rachel, who is now very calm

Margaret Don't worry. There must be some rational explanation.

Rachel No, there isn't. We're caught.

Dan comes downstairs, just as Edmund enters from the kitchen, carrying a large hammer

Dan Black as pitch. Nothing at all.

Edmund And the back door's the same as the front.

Dan So. That's that. We stay, and sit it out. Whatever it is.

Edmund Well, if it is some kind of mental force that's holding us here, let's see if it'll stand up to this. (*He holds up the hammer*)

Dan moves over to the drinks table

Dan I shall have a brandy. (*Looking at the bottle*) I hope . . . (*He pours himself a drink*)

Edmund These windows are made of perfectly ordinary glass. Nothing special, bullet-proof, or reinforced. Ordinary, breakable glass.

Dan (*sipping his brandy*) Mmmmmmmm. The brandy's O.K.

Edmund So a hammer should do the trick. (*He goes to the nearest window, and smashes the hammer hard against the glass. Nothing happens. Again, and again nothing*)

Rachel (*with a quiet smile*) No . . .

Dan (*sipping his brandy*) All I can say, is that we must be a very strong-minded lot. Anyone else want a drink?

Edmund moves to another window. He crashes the hammer against the glass, with the same lack of result. He throws the hammer on the floor, then sits dejectedly in a chair. There is a moment of silence

Edmund We can't get out.

They sit quite still and unmoving. Black-out
CURTAIN

ACT II

The same. A short while later

When the CURTAIN *rises, Margaret is seated, and Rachel is walking up and down in a restless manner. From upstairs there is a sporadic and intermittent sound of banging. Both women, for different reasons, are tense: but Margaret is trying hard to control her tension beneath her customary urbanity*

Almost immediately, Dan enters through the stairs door

Margaret What *is* he doing?

Dan Trying to see if it's possible to knock a house down from the inside. And failing. (*He pours himself a brandy*)

Margaret Of course he's failing. Logic should have told him that, without all this noise.

Dan Ed is a little bit low on logic at the moment. Panic might be a better word.

Margaret There's no need for you to be so superior. You're as scared as he is.

Dan Oh, I'm sure we're all terrified, but we do take it rather differently, don't we. You stand there mouthing nonsense about logic, whereas I, being a fatalist, withdraw into a stoical calm, Edmund tries to smash his way out with a cold chisel and a hammer, and Rachel walks up and down.

Margaret No, you talk, superficially and incessantly: and guzzle other people's brandy.

Dan It's a bit like the *Titanic*, isn't it. Ed runs screaming to the Captain, and pleads on his knees for a lifeboat. While I lean on the rail like Noël Coward, dropping witticisms into the rising waves.

Margaret Is that what you call them?

Rachel I wish he'd stop banging. It won't make any difference.

Dan Well, he's had a go at smashing out all the window frames, violently assaulted the chimney-breast where it was bricked up, tried to take all the doors off their hinges, and hammered himself silly at the ceiling in a vain attempt to get out on to the roof. As far as I can see, the only result was some chipped paint, and scratches on the paper. Any minute now exhaustion should set in.

Margaret And what will it take to shut you up?

Dan Don't get scratchy, darling. Keep your cool.

Margaret Spare us then for five minutes, please.

The banging stops

Dan You don't mind me chattering on do you, Rachel?

Rachel stops walking and seems to listen. She has not heard Dan

Rachel Yes . . . There is something. Now the banging's stopped.
Dan What?
Rachel Something. A noise. I can't quite hear it yet. Can you hear a noise?
Dan No . . .
Margaret What sort of noise?
Dan I can hear Edmund coming downstairs.
Rachel No, something else, not that . . .

Edmund enters through the stairs door. He is in his shirt sleeves, dusty, sweaty and a little desperate from his sustained efforts

Edmund It's no good. Nothing will budge.
Margaret Of course not, did you expect it would?
Edmund I don't understand it.
Margaret If you can't break a window with a hammer, Ed, you certainly won't knock your way through a brick wall.
Edmund How do you know? How do you know what I can do till I try it?
Margaret It's a reasonable inference.
Edmund To hell with reasonable inferences! If there's a way out of here I'll find it.
Dan There isn't.
Edmund And the rest of you can sit about or talk or do whatever you please . . .
Dan We'll all sit open-mouthed, Ed, and admire your determination.
Edmund There's just one other possibility.
Margaret What's that?
Edmund The fireplace. The old chimney's blocked, at least the full width of it is, to create a proper draught. But if I take the hood off, there's still probably enough room to get up the flue and out on to the roof. I'll have to put the fire out.
Dan Oh, now wait a minute, look . . .!
Edmund What?
Dan It is the middle of winter, it was bloody cold driving down here!
Edmund I can't take the hood off with the fire still alight can I?
Dan Ed, there's no electricity, the central heating's dead, if you put the fire out we'll all freeze to death!
Edmund It's the only way I haven't tried, it's that or nothing.
Margaret Ed, it's pointless, don't you understand? If you can't hammer your way through glass or open unlocked doors, then whatever it is that's keeping us in here isn't a natural force subject to natural laws, is it? It stopped you every other way, and it'll stop you going up the chimney too.
Edmund I'll believe that when I see it. I'll get a bucket of water.
Dan Oh my God!
Margaret This is ridiculous.
Dan Got any spare overcoats and scarves, Rachel, we're going to need them.

Margaret Why the hell should we all be frozen because you can't think straight!

Edmund It's your logic that's at fault, Margaret, not mine. When I get that hood off, it's clear to open sky. There's nothing in between to stop me. No glass, no woodwork, no locks. Straight out on to the roof.

Margaret When you get the hood off.

Edmund Well, that's just a couple of screws.

Margaret So were the hinges.

Edmund You're wasting your time, I'm going to try it.

Dan It's the Empire-building spirit, darling, we can't win.

Rachel (*loudly across the argument*) Be quiet, everybody, be quiet!

Edmund What?

Rachel The noise. I can just hear it.

Dan What noise? Can you hear a noise?

Margaret No.

Rachel Listen. It's very faint. A long way off.

Pause. A distant rumbling can be heard very faintly

Edmund Yes.

They all hear it now, and stand quite still, listening, as it gradually becomes louder

Margaret Thunder?

Rachel No.

Edmund Voices . . .

Rachel Getting closer.

Dan Is it here or outside?

Margaret Or in our heads?

Dan In all four heads at once?

Margaret Why not?

Rachel No, it's in here, loud . . . oh, loud!

The noise is now loud, already painful to Rachel, increasingly so to the others

Edmund Is it a hurricane?

Margaret An earthquake?

Rachel Brickwork . . .

Dan What?

Rachel Collapsing! Oh . . .! (*She holds her head against the noise, partly shielding her ears, partly as though protecting it from falling rubble*)

Margaret It's bursting my eardrums . . .!

The noise becomes unendurably loud for a few seconds, and they cover their ears in pain. Then the noise stops quite suddenly, and immediately there is the sound of breaking glass, as one of the windows which Edmund hit with the hammer falls in. Rachel sees it, turning at once to look. The others recover very slowly from the noise

Edmund Dear God, I can still hear it . . .

Margaret Have you ever heard anything like that before?

Rachel Look at the window.
Edmund What?
Rachel It's broken.

Without a word Edmund goes to the window. Dan and Margaret follow him

Didn't you hear? (*She sits down*)
Edmund It is. It's broken.
Margaret But the glass is on the floor. So it must have been broken from the outside.
Dan A stone?
Edmund Or a bullet?
Dan Good God, that's all we need, someone taking pot shots at us!
Margaret It can't be a bullet or a stone. It's not starred at all.
Dan Ed's hammer must have cracked it?
Margaret Yes, and the noise shook it out.
Dan That's right.
Edmund So we can get out. Can't we? Look. There's no glass there now, is there?
Margaret But it's still pitch black.
Dan I can't feel any cold air. Can you?
Margaret No.
Edmund But you can see it can't you, you can see it the same as I can! It's broken, the glass is gone, it's there, on the floor! So the blackness, that must be the night air. It must be!
Dan Come on then, Ed. The honour is yours.
Margaret There's just room to get your hand through.

Pause. They all look at Edmund, including Rachel, as he puts his hand through the broken window. He stops, after a few seconds, and withdraws his hand. He looks at the others

Edmund (*ashen*) I can't.
Margaret What?
Edmund There's something in the way.
Dan What?
Edmund I don't know.
Dan Can you feel it?
Edmund No. I can't feel anything. But I can't get my hand through. Not an inch.
Margaret Q.E.D.

Pause

Rachel (*quietly*) It isn't the night air.
Edmund What?
Rachel There's no moon.
Edmund No.
Rachel Nor any stars.
Edmund No, it's still pitch black.

Rachel Where are we then, where there's no moon and the stars have gone
out?
Edmund We're here in our cottage. Where we've always been.
Rachel Yes, we're in the cottage. But that's not the night air.

Pause. They are all disconcerted by Rachel

Dan Well then, what now, Ed? You're the commander of this little
expedition.
Edmund I don't know.
Dan How about putting the fire out and climbing up the chimney? There's
· nothing in the way. It's clear to open sky.
Edmund (*angrily*) For God's sake, what's the point of sneering? You
sound as if you're glad. Do you want to stay in here?
Dan Not in the least. But I know when I'm beaten.
Edmund Well I'm not. Not yet, not by a long way.
Dan I admit, I do have a rather low surrender threshold, and am prone to
total collapse the moment the pressure is on. But as a tactic, I can
recommend it. It does have the virtue of leaving your opponent com-
pletely bemused by the ease of his victory.
Margaret What opponent?
Dan Yes, that's a good point.
Edmund Listen, supposing we try to work out what's likely to happen
next? There's probably some kind of a pattern in everything that's
happened so far, and if we can find it . . .
Dan Supposing nothing does?
Edmund What?
Dan Supposing nothing happens? Supposing that dreadful noise was the
last of it, and now we just sit here? Just shut in, and that's that. There's
logic in that too. After all, we've just had a very effective demonstration
of the fact that we're not going to get out of here by any natural method,
haven't we?
Edmund Something's bound to happen sooner or later.
Dan Why?
Edmund Well, because . . .
Dan A totally unjustified assumption. Perhaps this is the end now. Just
the four of us, and time, and silence.
Rachel (*very quietly*) And the house . . .

*There is a bleak pause, Edmund's energy momentarily sapped, Dan and
Margaret feeling the full implications of what has just been said. Rachel is
intensely self-absorbed, and only half with the conversation. With a conscious
effort Margaret breaks the mood*

Margaret (*briskly*) All right. Calmly and rationally. Let's work it out.
Rachel (*half to herself*) It's a waste of time.
Dan Why not just sit back and enjoy it? After all, in a sense, we're
privileged. We're experiencing something that's probably unique.
Margaret That's just the point. In a situation like this, none of us has any

experience to draw on. So we do what we've done before. We try all the
physical solutions, the doors and the windows.
Dan Don't look at me, I haven't tried anything except the brandy.
Margaret But clearly that's the wrong tactic, because it doesn't work.
Instead of using our hands, we should have been using our brains.
Edmund And where will that get us? Only back here, inside the same
physical situation.
Margaret Or will it? Well, let's try it and see. So, inside the house,
several extraordinary things have happened that we can't explain except
by suggesting that we're all sharing the same hysterical delusion.
Dan I'm glad I married a rationalist. I always knew it would come in
useful.
Margaret But now the house itself has become part of the delusion. We
look through the windows, and see nothing, and some inexplicable force
keeps the doors closed. The same force keeps us inside, even when a
window is broken.
Edmund (*to himself*) The house itself . . . ? (*He walks away by himself to a
corner*)

*Margaret moves over to Dan, and speaks to him urgently, and semi-
privately*

Margaret What do you think is beyond those walls, Dan? Outside the
door? Do you think it's the two cars, and a patch of grass, with a track
leading to the main road? Or is it something else? . . . Just space,
perhaps?
Dan If it's just space, your rationality's wearing a bit thin.

*Margaret moves away from him, glancing down at her watch. As she does so,
she stops, and looks up at the clock on the wall*

Margaret What time does your watch say?
Dan Five thirty. It's stopped.
Margaret Edmund?
Edmund Five thirty.
Margaret Rachel?
Rachel (*without looking*) Five thirty.
Margaret So does mine. So does the electric clock. And I bet you every
other clock in the house says five thirty too.
Edmund That must have been the time when the lights went out.
Margaret So. Everything stopped at five thirty.
Edmund Or started . . .
Dan Everything?
Margaret (*half to herself*) And I wonder what time it is now?
Dan For a rationalist, you're getting very fanciful. I'd prefer to wait and
see before venturing into the realms of science fiction. After all, we're
perfectly O.K., nothing's happening to us. At the moment.
Edmund (*returning to the group*) It's the house, I'm sure it's something to
do with the house. It all began when the house ceased functioning.

Margaret The machinery, not the house. It may be that the house is functioning perfectly well.
Rachel (*quietly*) I think we've been selected.

Complete silence. Rachel is sitting very upright and still, and the strength and simplicity of her words strikes them all silent

Edmund What do you mean?
Rachel Chosen. In some way. The four of us.
Margaret What for?
Dan Something nice, I hope.
Rachel No . . . I don't think so.

Edmund is thinking furiously

Margaret (*slightly irritated*) Well, we don't achieve anything by getting all intense and visionary about it, do we. What we need is to keep our eyes open and our minds at full stretch; and whatever we find happening to us, try to understand it.
Dan Our antennae you mean. You always have put too much reliance on the intellect. You look at Rachel. She's got all her receivers working at full power. It's nothing to do with the intellect, what's registering on her.

Dan and Margaret look at Rachel, sitting unnaturally still, and beginning to sweat on her forehead

Margaret You want to believe it, don't you, that's what it is. But I don't. I want to *know!*

A slight pause. Edmund moves back into the conversation

Edmund If it is something to do with the house, it can't be the house on its own, can it?
Margaret And what's that supposed to mean?
Dan Personally, I've always thought that houses were places you lived in, not malevolent spirits, locking their doors and reinforcing their windows at you whenever they feel like it.
Edmund It must be *us* as well. Us and the house, together.

Slight pause

Dan I don't think I feel any special point of contact with houses of any kind, Ed, evil-minded or not. I certainly wouldn't enter into a conspiracy with one to lock myself inside it.
Edmund Don't you see what I mean? Margaret said that the only way we can make sense of what's happening to us here is to say that it's something our four minds have created between them. But there's the house too; the house is crucial. It must be! It's some co-ordination or co-incidence between the four of us, and this place, some accidental arrangement of presences, like the one correct combination of tumblers that will open a safe. Don't you understand?
Margaret (*quietly*) Really, Ed, it's getting ridiculous, isn't it.
Edmund I don't see why?

Margaret We might just as well start blaming wizards and magicians. If we don't stick to what has actually happened, and what we know, if we start indulging personal fantasies . . .

Edmund It isn't fantasy . . .

Margaret Then we'll very soon lose whatever sense of reality we might have left.

Edmund You yourself said it, the house itself has become part of our hysterical delusion . . .

Margaret Yes, I know, Ed, I said that: but it was just a wild hypothesis, that's all. Does anybody take it at all seriously?

Edmund All right then, hard facts. Did you have pains in your belly or not?

Margaret Yes, I had pains in my belly.

Edmund And did you hear music?

Margaret Yes, I heard music.

Edmund And can you get out of here now?

Margaret No, I can't get out.

Edmund So what are you going to do about it?

Dan *I'm* not going to do anything about it. I'm going to sit here and drink brandy and wait till it's morning.

Edmund Morning? What do you mean, morning? What makes you think it's going to get light out there? That isn't night, outside the window. That's blackness, absolute blackness! All the clocks have stopped, all the watches too. So what time is it, Dan? Can you tell me the time?

Dan No, I can't tell you the time, Ed.

Edmund How long will it be till morning then? And how long has it been since all those things happened? Two hours or twenty minutes, can you tell?

Dan No, I can't tell.

Margaret Calm down, Ed, there's no need to get worked up.

Edmund Oh yes there is, there's a hell of a need to get worked up! I'm going to get out of here some way or another. I'm not going to sit on my bum with a brandy in my hand and wait and see what happens. There's something we've missed somewhere, some loophole in the argument we haven't spotted, something that will make it all clear. And once it is clear what has happened, we'll know what action to take to get us out . . . If you've got any better ideas I'd like to hear them.

Margaret No, Ed. We haven't got any better ideas.

Short pause

Edmund And I'll tell you another hard fact too.

Margaret What's that?

Edmund If it is some combination of the house and ourselves . . . (*he looks at them*) . . . well. I've been here with Rachel dozens of times. We've had friends here for the week-end too, on at least two occasions. But you, Dan, and Margaret, you've not been here before.

Margaret So?

Edmund Well. That makes one point of difference, doesn't it. Something about this gathering that's unique. The house, Rachel and myself, and you two.

Pause

Dan Well. That's charming of you, Ed.

Margaret (*in disbelief*) Are you trying to say that somehow, all this is our fault?

Edmund Not your fault alone, no.

Dan That's jolly decent of you.

Edmund I'm not saying that at all. But you two are the new element in the situation. So it could be something about you—or rather, about you and us together . . . And if we want to get out of here, I think we'd better sit down and examine ourselves and the situation between us, rather honestly.

Pause. Dan and Margaret can hardly believe their ears

Dan Well, I was briefly a member of the Communist Party, Ed, when I was at college. It's probably that.

Edmund Take it seriously, Dan, please, this is a serious situation.

Dan Take it seriously, how can I begin to take it seriously when you insist in turning the whole thing into a ridiculous joke? What do you want us to do, sit down and have a true confessions session, drag out all our little peccadilloes and misdemeanours, till a sepulchral voice booms out "He's the one!" and drags one of us down to hell like Don Giovanni?

Edmund (*irritably*) No, of course not, I don't mean that!

Dan Retribution went out a long time ago. If there's one thing we've learned this century, it's that the biggest crooks usually get away with it.

Edmund Of course I didn't mean that, I didn't say that, you know I didn't! Why must you turn everything into a joke?

Margaret It's a hopeless task, Ed, even if it were feasible. The number of possibilities is enormous, we'd need a computer.

Edmund No, no, it's a simple answer, I'm quite sure, something simple and logical we haven't spotted.

Dan Why be so arrogant as to assume an answer, there may not be one. It might be one of those stimulating mysteries like the *Marie Celeste*, where no-one will ever know.

Edmund Dan, why must you be so infuriatingly flippant? After all, you were the one talking about all this earlier tonight!

Dan Was I?

Edmund The submerged energy of the mind, and powers beyond the rational—you were making great efforts to convince us then!

Margaret Games with ice cubes, darling.

Dan Oh yes, all that.

Edmund The world that lives in us, in spite of us.

Dan That'll teach me to keep some control over my party conversation, won't it.

Edmund That's what's happened, you see, you've hit it, Dan!

Dan Have I?

Edmund The world that lives in us! How would it be if that world in some way took over? If the inner world and the outer world changed places?

Dan In my case it would be disastrous. My day to day life is shambles enough, my inner life is total chaos!

Margaret Mine's rather vicious. All the old scores I could pay off, as part of the natural order of things!

Edmund So that the ordinary external world, the world of physical reality, becomes subservient to the world of dreams and desires! That's it, you see? That's why I'm right! It's us! We've done it! We've projected something in ourselves, out of ourselves, till it's become fact. You said exactly that, Margaret, about the African carving. In the imagination desires become facts, what you want becomes real!

Dan In that case, what nasty imaginations we do have.

Margaret Drinking blood and dead children! A very turbulent and greasy pool inside one of us!

Edmund But which one?

Margaret What do you mean, which one?

Edmund What I say. Which one?

Dan You're not serious are you?

Edmund Of course I'm serious!

Pause

Margaret Forget it, Ed, it's nonsense: one of the biggest clichés of science fiction. You read it somewhere.

Edmund No, I didn't read it! I mean it!

Dan Look, Ed, I suggest you sit down quietly somewhere, and let your imagination cool down a bit. You're getting a bit overheated.

Edmund No, no, I'm not, I can see it now. I can see through all this pretence!

Margaret The worst thing we can do in this situation is to get caught up in our own fantasies. We ought to stay very dull and prosaic and down to earth. It may be boring, but it's safer.

Dan What pretence, Ed?

Edmund You and Margaret. The game you're playing.

Margaret What game?

Dan Are you playing a game, darling? I'm not. As far as I know.

Edmund Why are you both so resolutely determined not to be serious? Why do you both refuse to look this business in the face? Every time I get near to what's happening, you two try to head me off, you try every trick you know to keep me away from the truth!

Dan This is ridiculous.

Margaret What truth?

Edmund That it's you, of course, one of you two! Or perhaps both of you. None of this has ever happened before. Neither of you has been here before either, and all the time you try to laugh it off.

Rachel looks slowly round at Edmund. Dan and Margaret are totally at a loss now, not sure whether to be amused or offended

Dan Ed, don't be silly.

Edmund I'm not being silly. I'm being very practical. I want to get out of here. I'm going to get out too, neither one of you is going to stop me!

Rachel stands up and speaks very strongly

Rachel Ed, be quiet!
Edmund What . . .?
Margaret Rachel . . .?
Dan I thought she was asleep.
Edmund Rachel, don't you see it . . .?
Rachel I see you making a fool of yourself.
Edmund It must be them, who else can it be?
Rachel It could as easily be me. It could be you.
Edmund Me? How could it be me? Do I want us to stay here in this madhouse?
Rachel You've hated this house from the first. That's why you spent so much money on it. That's why we've almost crippled ourselves, always the most modern and the most expensive of everything. It's like the whipping boy, a way of punishing yourself.
Edmund That's not true, Rachel . . .
Rachel I didn't see it at the beginning, but it became obvious after a while. You didn't want a cottage in the country, so you bought the most dilapidated one we could find. You felt uneasy about your own comfort, so you turned it into a show place. You felt ashamed of spending so much money, so you jumped at every opportunity of spending more. You're still not at ease here, so you keep inviting people down in the hope that they'll convince you.
Edmund (*pale and shattered*) Don't say any more.
Rachel Now your own guilt tells you it must be your fault, punishment inflicted on all of us because of you. But you can't bear that, so you lose your temper and turn on your friends. You try to avoid accusing yourself by accusing them.
Edmund No!
Rachel It's very simple, and rather sad, to someone who loves you.
Edmund Do you really think of me like that?
Rachel I understand you, and I know how you feel. I know how real it is, and how much it hurts. But I can't let you make a fool of yourself by savaging our friends.

Edmund is totally reduced, all energy drained

Edmund What can I say . . .?

Pause

Margaret There's no need to worry. No offence taken.
Dan We can truthfully say, I think, that we are all under some strain.

Pause

Rachel We should leave each other alone. We've done nothing.
Margaret What?

Rachel It's not to do with what we've done. What we are.

Margaret What do you mean by that?

Rachel What we are . . . (*She stops speaking, as though mesmerized by what she has said and sits down, rather abruptly*)

Rachel's straight-backed figure absorbs Margaret and Dan for a few seconds. Edmund though, is still too embarrassed to recognize fully the processes happening within her

Edmund I ought to apologize. But I don't know where to begin.

Dan Don't bother. We'll take it as read.

Edmund I suppose I knew I had all that inside me. In my honester moments. I'm pretty horrified it came out so viciously.

Dan Oh, for God's sake, don't be horrified! Self-flagellation is a very overrated pastime. Particularly the mental kind.

Edmund (*ruefully*) Some people are born with it, I think.

Margaret Everyone thinks vicious thoughts about their friends. It's one of the things friends are for.

Edmund Not everybody says them though.

Dan For instance, our jealousy as you were showing us around the place was so overwhelming it must have been almost tangible. I felt bright green.

Edmund Don't . . .

As Dan speaks, Margaret's attention is re-attracted by Rachel, still sitting bright-eyed and rigid on the sofa

Dan Here am I, I was thinking, having sold out every shred of integrity and talent years ago, and here's Ed, still fighting grim battles with his conscience. And he lives like this, while I kip down in a kind of intellectual Rowton House! I feel a bit like Faust being told that Helen of Troy's gone back to her husband, and all the Kingdoms of the earth have become republics.

Edmund Dan, I envy you your ability to joke about it.

Margaret Rachel . . .?

Dan It's a mark of the useless intellect, Ed, the unemployed mind. It searches for the amusing angle on everything because it has nothing better to do. A bit like doing crosswords.

Rachel begins to sway slightly

Margaret (*becoming concerned*) Rachel, are you all right?

Rachel No, I don't think so . . .

Edmund What?

Margaret Look at her.

Edmund What's the matter?

Margaret She's very pale. And soaking wet.

Rachel I feel so hot. I can't breathe . . .!

Edmund crosses to her, and supports her with his arm round her shoulder

Edmund All right darling, there, take deep breaths . . .

Rachel I can't, I can't breathe . . . Oh my God . . .!
Margaret Dan, get a glass of water.

Dan goes to the table and pours out a glass of water

Rachel It's so hot!
Margaret I think she's going to faint.
Edmund Hold on darling, there's a drink coming.

Rachel slumps limply in Edmund's arms

Dan Here. (*He tries to hold the glass to her lips, but the water runs down her chin*)
Margaret Don't pour it all over her!
Dan I can't help it . . .
Edmund She's gone.
Dan She's flat out.
Margaret Just a minute. (*She wets a handkerchief in the water and dabs Rachel's forehead with it*)
Edmund It's no good. She's right out. She's gone completely limp.
Dan Is it a faint?
Margaret It looked like a faint. Hot and short of breath.
Edmund (*slapping her face lightly*) Rachel, Rachel . . .
Dan That won't do it. She's really out.
Margaret Hang on.
Dan What?
Margaret I've got some smelling-salts in my bag.
Dan I didn't know you carried smelling-salts. What a sweet old-fashioned thing to do.
Margaret It's for all our friends. When you bore them into insensibility.
Dan Ah.
Edmund It doesn't look like a faint. She's fast asleep.
Margaret Well . . .

She puts the salts bottle under Rachel's nose. Rachel groans and rolls her head away, but shows no sign of waking. Dan and Margaret are slightly nonplussed

Dan Oh.
Margaret Mmm. She really is out. Smelling salts usually do the trick.
Edmund Again.

Margaret tries the salts again. Rachel reacts with groans and movement, but does not wake. Uncertainty and the beginning of fear is stirring in all three characters. It is most obvious in Edmund, but present too in Margaret and Dan, though their characters lead them to hide it or play it down

Margaret No. That's not going to work.
Edmund If it is a faint, she should be coming round by now.
Dan It does look more like sleep.
Margaret Her breathing is very quiet, listen.

They listen for a moment

Dan Barely audible.
Edmund I can still feel it though. Not deep, but regular . . . Do you think she's all right?
Margaret I don't know. It's very odd.
Edmund Oh my God . . . I think she's dying.
Dan Dying?
Edmund The breathing. It feels very faint now.
Margaret Lay her down quickly! Lay her down flat!

With great urgency they arrange Rachel on the sofa

Edmund Rachel!
Margaret Don't panic, just get her as comfortable as possible.
Edmund What on earth can have happened to her? Could it be a heart attack, or a stroke?
Margaret I don't think so. She didn't say anything about pain, and her colour was all wrong for a heart attack.
Dan She's breathing perfectly well now. You get very close and listen. It's faint, but perfectly regular.
Margaret (*feeling Rachel's pulse*) So is her pulse too, feel.

Edmund feels Rachel's pulse. Its inexplicable steadiness adds to the fear in the air

Edmund My God, what's happened to her?
Margaret I don't think she's ill. Look at her.
Dan She's fast asleep, that's all. Flat out to the world.
Margaret It must be a nervous reaction of some kind. I mean why not. She looks perfectly peaceful now.
Edmund Except . . .
Margaret What?
Edmund None of these things are natural, are they.
Margaret Well, I don't know about that.
Edmund Oh come on, Margaret, you've been tying your mind in knots trying to think of a rational way out, when it gets clearer and clearer there isn't one!
Margaret I reserve judgement on that.
Dan And if it's not rational, what then?
Edmund Then this is a part of it too. The sleeping. Perhaps it's the beginning.
Dan The beginning of what?
Edmund Which of us will feel short of breath next, and then go unconscious, all in a few seconds? Who will be the third one? And what will the last one do, with three of us sleeping, and only himself, or herself awake?
Margaret That's absurdly melodramatic.
Edmund No it isn't. Don't you feel a kind of terror closing in? Like ice, building up all round us?
Margaret It's getting colder, certainly.
Edmund Yes it is, but I don't mean that. I mean terror.

There is a moment of silence in the candlelit gloom, the three figures, the body on the sofa, darkness and emptiness. But such feelings offend Margaret, and she has to break them

Margaret (*shaken*) Ed, you have a talent for histrionics that has lain dormant all these years. It's perfectly plain what's happened. Rachel, after a period of high nervous excitement, including a row with you, has fallen into a deep and refreshing sleep. Look at her! She's stopped sweating, her colour's back to normal. She's fast asleep, and jolly good luck to her. I wish I was!

Edmund If it's just sleep, it ought to be perfectly possible to wake her up, then? By shaking her, or shouting in her ear?

Margaret (*troubled*) No. I wouldn't do that.

Edmund Why wouldn't you?

Margaret It's always bad to startle people from sleep like that.

Edmund (*with a kind of triumph*) If it is sleep.

Pause. A sense of helplessness. Dan picks the situation up

Dan Well, I think we're all becoming victims of Ed's obsessions.

Edmund When I said that, you laughed at me.

Dan I don't mean supernaturally, Ed, nothing could be more prosaic. Fathers and sons. All those inherited burdens we carry to the graveside, then pass on to our children with a wicked little smile.

Edmund I don't know what you're talking about.

Dan I think you've got your old man shut up in a cupboard somewhere, and he's putting the evil eye on us till you let him out.

Edmund Oh Dan, really!

Dan Or to put it another way, Ed, there are things locked up in you which lead you to put the worst construction on things.

Edmund Is it me then, all this, have I done it?

Dan No, you haven't dear man, and that's the point! Margaret and myself you see, being to all intents and purposes angels of light, and of the most crystalline and unclouded conscience, we tend to adopt a more hopeful frame of mind, and assume the best, not the worst. Which is why I suggest you stop lacerating yourself and us, and just let things happen for a bit. Regard them with appreciation or amazement, if you must, but don't necessarily assume they're directed personally at you! And now, I have a quite revolutionary suggestion to make.

Edmund What?

Dan Let's all go to bed. Then when we wake up it'll be Boxing Day morning, and we can all have a huge breakfast, because by then we'll be starving.

Margaret Dan, that is a very good idea!

Dan Of course it is, don't sound so amazed. It's like marital rows or worries about your career. When they happen in the middle of the night, ignore them, because it all looks quite different in the morning. So, where shall we sleep?

Edmund You can if you like. I'll stay here with Rachel.

Margaret Well I certainly don't intend to sleep upstairs, Ed!

Edmund Because of the room?

Margaret What?

Edmund The bedroom. Where Rachel saw the child.

Margaret Oh, no. I'd forgotten that. No, because it'll be freezing cold up there without central heating, that's why.

Dan It's getting cold enough down here.

Margaret We'll make up a marital couch by the fire, shall we, darling? How do you fancy snuggling down by the embers?

Dan It'll be like returning to my earliest youth. I had my first meaningful experiences on hearthrugs.

Margaret Not with me you didn't.

Dan You were still at school. So was I, come to that.

Margaret Where are the blankets, Ed?

Edmund They're in the room too. There's a built in blanket cupboard, opposite the bed.

Margaret Well, if you don't mind me pinching a candle, I'll go up and get them.

Edmund Margaret . . .

Margaret What?

Edmund The room. Do you mind?

Margaret Mind? Why on earth should I mind?

Dan Shall I come with you?

Margaret No. If I want any help, I'll call you . . . To carry the blankets I mean.

Margaret exits upstairs carrying a candle

Dan Margaret's as tough as old boots you know, she really is. That's why I adore her . . . Rachel still asleep?

Edmund Exactly the same.

Dan Strange. But very sensible in the circumstances. I don't like it, so I'll sleep it out. Admirable.

Edmund I wonder if she's dreaming? And what about?

Dan It'd have to be pretty exotic to cap this. What do you dream if life becomes a nightmare? Peace perhaps.

Pause. Edmund is very subdued, sitting by Rachel, holding her unresponsive hand

Edmund You're right about me, Dan. And Rachel, of course.

Dan Right about what?

Edmund The legacy I get from my father. Whether I like it or not.

Dan Not only you.

Edmund It's a bit much to be loaded with a Puritan conscience when you're not a Puritan.

Dan Oh my dear man, half the population could say the same thing! They all parade about proclaiming their intellectual freedom and moral liberty, and just behind their shoulder comes this grim-faced chap with a tall black hat and a white collar.

Edmund Where's yours then?

Dan In my case he shrivelled. You need to preserve some moral sense, or the poor bugger starves to death.

Edmund I don't believe you.

Dan Don't deceive yourself into thinking that I'm very good-hearted under this glittering exterior! I tried to comfort myself with that thought till I was nearly thirty. I was preserving my real and worthwhile self to blossom in middle age. Now I'm on the verge of middle age, I find there's nothing left to blossom with. The bud has gone rotten, and the whole tree is dying, from the root up.

Edmund That's just self-dramatization.

Dan Maybe. (*He gives a rather frosty smile*)

A silence descends. Edmund looks down at Rachel and speaks quietly

Edmund But she knows me, you see. All my evasions and self-deceptions. Even if I hide them from myself, I can't hide them from her. (*He gets up, and looks round at the house*) All this, for instance. It's wrong, I know that.

Dan All what?

Edmund The house. Me. Us.

Dan Ah.

Edmund I know what price the rest of the world pays for our comfort: and how many thin Africans it takes to make one overweight Englishman. And that knowledge is the beginning of damnation.

Dan Fruitless, Ed. Fruitless luxury.

Edmund Luxury?

Dan You don't intend to do anything about it, any more than anyone else does. Agonizing over it gives you the double satisfaction of feeling bad about it, and feeling good about feeling bad, both at the same time.

Edmund Yes. That's right too I suppose.

Dan Of course it's right. We're all dab hands at these games with conscience, our generation. We grew up with them.

Edmund But I'm also good at my job! Very good at it! I make a lot of money, and I'm capable of making a lot more. (*Viciously*) Why the hell shouldn't I? There are enough incapable people in the world, but I'm not one of them! I can cope!

Dan Now now.

Edmund What?

Dan Not content with being the big bad wolf, you want to be the ogre that eats children as well. Forget it. Have a drink.

Edmund Yes. I think I will.

Dan The brandy is very reliable. Smooth and strong and uncompromised. Like me.

Edmund (*pouring himself a drink*) It's very strange to be standing here, drinking brandy and talking so rationally . . . (*Looking back at Rachel*) Over my wife's body.

Dan Her sleeping body.

Edmund Are you frightened, Dan?

Dan Terrified my dear! I'm keeping my aplomb, that's all.

Edmund Every now and then I get a great surge of feeling that everything must be all right really. The doors are open and we imagined it all. Standing here talking to you it's very hard to believe any of it happened.

Dan Try the red wine.

Edmund No . . . I can't do that.

Dan Then we'd better assume everything did. Or our perception problems will get even worse than they are.

Edmund What will happen to us?

Dan I don't choose to think about that. I'm a slave to experience, Ed, a creature of the present moment. It's the only way life can be made endurable. Otherwise it consists of nothing but regrets over the past and apprehensions about the future. Who wants to live like that?

Edmund No-one.

Dan That's right. No-one.

Edmund speaks quietly but suddenly, without preparation, as if what he says is always ready in his mind

Edmund When I won my scholarship, my dad said to me, "Eddie my son, your father was born and brought up in a slum street in the East End, and he's wasted his life in dirty factories making other people rich. And now, you're going to Oxford. Through you son, and others like you, the working class will come to power." Even at eighteen, I didn't know where to look.

Dan is embarrassed and looks at his feet. The silence is broken by the sound of Margaret's feet coming downstairs, quite fast

Dan Mmmm. Sounds like she made it.

Margaret enters from the stairs door, carrying a pile of blankets and the candle. She looks white and strained, but tries to give no sign of it, busying herself with the candle, and taking the blankets across to the fire

Hello, darling . . . All well?

Margaret Yes, all well . . . How's Rachel?

Edmund Just the same.

Margaret Here, take these. My arms are breaking.

Dan goes to help her with the blankets

Dan Good God! Your hands!

Margaret What?

Dan They're freezing! Like ice.

Margaret Of course they are. It's cold up there.

Dan And you're shaking. You're shaking like a leaf!

Margaret All right then. I'm shaking.

Edmund goes to her.

Edmund What happened?

Margaret Nothing happened. I got cold.

Edmund I think something did.

Margaret (*strongly*) All right, I was scared stiff, I was scared out of my wits, are you satisfied? But nothing happened. I saw nothing, I touched nothing, nothing happened!

Edmund But you were scared stiff.

Margaret That was my own fault, my imagination running riot, that's all. Like everything else in this God awful place! Why the hell can't we be adding machines, just get the facts, and store them, and that's that. Why the hell do we have to dramatize everything!

Dan Tell me, darling.

Margaret It was nothing, Dan, I was just scared, that's all. I was alone, in the dark, there were shadows and noises, and I was scared.

Dan Noises?

Edmund What noises?

Margaret I don't know, it's all nonsense.

Edmund What noises?

Margaret Breathing. Breathing noises. It was me, obviously I was listening to my own breathing, and it frightened me.

Edmund Tell us what happened.

Margaret I told you, nothing happened! . . . I just went upstairs to get the blankets. The candle didn't throw much light, but I could see perfectly well. I found the cupboard with no trouble at all, and I opened it. The bed was behind me.

Dan And then?

Margaret And then I—I felt I wasn't alone. I can't explain it any more than that. There was someone else, other people, in the room with me. And that's when I heard the breathing. Or thought I heard it. Coming from the bed, behind me.

Dan What sort of breathing?

Margaret Difficult. Laboured.

Edmund It couldn't have been you then.

Margaret I turned round, and of course, there was nothing. It was just the room. I stood there, quite detached. I said to myself, "All right Margaret, this is fascinating, you're going to stare this one out, whatever it is, you're going to look it in the face, study it and observe your own reactions." So I just stood there with the blankets and the candle, for what seemed like a long time. But then . . .

Dan What?

Margaret I don't really know. I had to leave, that's all. I had to come downstairs. Get out of that room.

Dan Dear God, rather you than me.

Margaret It was imagination, Dan, it was my imagination. What else could it be?

Dan I think that's a question we don't ask any more.

Margaret Anyway, I'm all right, aren't I! I'm not shaking. My hands are getting warmer.

At this point they are all facing Margaret and Rachel is behind them. Slowly, without waking, she sits up on the sofa. Her eyes are closed, but her mouth is moving soundlessly, and there is an expression of terror on her face

Dan A bit warmer.

Margaret Well, whatever else happened, it was damn cold up there. Below zero I should think.

Dan rubs Margaret's hands, and they snuggle in a semi-embrace. Edmund turns away from them, and sees Rachel. Her face is contorted with agony, but completely without sound or bodily movement. Edmund watches for a few seconds, horror-stricken

Edmund (*quietly*) Look at Rachel.

Dan and Margaret both turn and look, and like Edmund are struck to silence by what they see. There is a pause, and they too speak quietly

Margaret Is she asleep or awake?

Edmund She's trying to say something.

Dan She's in agony!

Margaret She's dreaming. She must be dreaming.

Dan Dreaming what, for heaven's sake, to make her look like that?

Quite suddenly, Rachel gives a little grunt and her eyes open. She is awake, still sitting up, and with no trace of the fear or agony

Rachel Umm ... Oh ... Oh ... Hallo ... Um ... I must have fallen asleep.

Edmund Rachel!

Edmund moves quickly across to her, and half embraces her. The other two watch keenly

Rachel Oh ... What's the matter, Ed? ... I'm a bit dizzy.

Edmund Do you feel all right?

Rachel Of course I feel all right ... Not awake yet.

Edmund You fell asleep very suddenly.

Rachel Did I? I don't remember. Just that I felt tired.

Dan Did you dream anything?

Rachel No. I don't think so. Not that I can remember.

Margaret How do you feel? Not ill or anything?

Rachel No. What's wrong? Why do you keep asking me questions? I feel just as I felt before. Except a bit colder.

Dan Have a blanket.

Rachel Blankets?

Dan Margaret got them when you were asleep. (*He hands Rachel a blanket*)

Margaret We thought we might go to sleep too. It doesn't seem such a good idea now though.

Rachel Nothing's changed has it?

Edmund No. Nothing's changed.

Rachel No. It still feels the same. (*She gets up, and winds the blanket*

*around her, almost like a shawl. She begins to walk slowly around the
room, looking at it, and then touching the walls, as though measuring or
describing them)*

Edmund watches her

Dan (*to Margaret, quietly*) So what now?
Margaret (*quietly*) God knows. Perhaps we all go quite crazy. After all,
what's happened? Rachel fell asleep on the sofa and I got frightened of
the dark. Is that any reason for panic?
Dan There were other things, if you remember.
Margaret Yes dear. I remember.
Dan Shall we make up this bed then?
Margaret If you like. Not in front of the fire though. That would be a bit
too anti-social, even for us.

*They take some blankets down stage to a point opposite the sofa, and begin
to arrange them. Dan looks up and notices Rachel's strange perambulation
round the room, which Edmund is avidly following*

Dan Just a minute. Look.
Margaret What?
Dan Look at her.

They watch her uncertainly, not knowing what to say

Edmund Rachel, what are you doing?
Rachel Doing? I'm not doing anything.
Edmund Walking round the room like that. Touching things.
Rachel Oh. Am I? I didn't notice. I still feel rather dizzy actually. And sort
of claustrophobic.
Edmund Claustrophobic?
Rachel Shut in. I don't know.
Edmund Come and sit down.
Rachel (*shivering*) Oh, yes. I'm still quite cold. It's a good thing we've got
the fire.

*Rachel sits with Edmund on the sofa quite close to the fire. He puts his arms
round her to warm her*

Dan (*quietly*) Shut in! She can say that again.
Rachel Oh, that's better. That's nice.
Edmund When you were asleep—did you feel anything? I mean, did
anything happen?
Rachel What can happen when you're asleep?
Edmund And you didn't dream anything?
Rachel I told you, I can never remember dreams. I'm fine now. Just this
dizziness from waking up.
Dan (*to Margaret; quietly*) So there.

*Most of the dramatic emphasis now falls on Dan and Margaret, down stage
with their half-made bed*

Margaret She doesn't remember.

Dan Give in gracefully, darling. You can't expect to find a rational answer where none of the laws of reason apply.

Margaret We don't know that, that's just an assumption on your part. You've always been a great one for that: when you can't understand something, make an unjustified assumption, and announce it as fact.

Dan Ah, that's one of the benefits of a university education. Two useful things I learned at college: whatever you say is true, if you say it authoritatively enough. And don't worry if you haven't read the books everyone's talking about, because they haven't read them either.

Pause. Margaret looks apprehensively round at the candlelight and silence

Margaret Dan, we're in trouble, aren't we.

Dan Not at this precise moment, as far as I can see. Everything's rather placid.

Margaret It really hit me upstairs in the room. For the first time.

Dan I've been to better Christmas parties, certainly. I've been to worse, too, now I come to think of it.

Margaret (*smiling wanly*) Shall I tell you one of the things I love about you?

Dan Tell me more than one, or I shall begin to despair.

Margaret You're relentless. Most people know when to stop, but you don't. You just plough on, don't you.

Dan Is that a virtue?

Margaret Tonight it is.

Pause

Dan Stop thinking about it. There's nothing you can do.

Margaret I can't help it. I was born that way. I've often thought, when I die, I'd hate to be drugged into insensibility. However painful it is. I shall want to know, as long as I can. Die with my eyes open. (*After a pause*) George Orwell said it's best to die in your boots.

Dan *He* didn't.

Margaret No.

They both fall silent in thought for a moment

Edmund Do you feel better now?

Rachel Yes, fine. I wonder how long we'll have to wait?

Edmund Wait? What for?

Rachel I don't know. But I'm sure we're waiting for something. (*She listens to the silence*)

Margaret Do you feel responsible at all?

Dan In general, or today?

Margaret For all this.

Dan How can I, when I don't know what it is?

Margaret I don't. Ed sees the fate of the whole universe depending on whether or not he's saved, but that's alien to me. I've always been totally convinced of my own innocence.

Dan I hope you don't go to heaven. I shall miss you.

Margaret No, you're not one of the goats, Dan. You've never done anything positive enough for hell.

Dan There I must disagree with you. I'm sure the cabinet posts, as it were, in the great republic of the damned, are held by the Stalins and Hitlers, and that the murderers, liars and betrayers make a very efficient Civil Service. But your average goat, the rank and file of the underworld, I'm pretty sure that's made up of shallow nonentities like me.

Margaret (*hurt*) Don't say that.

Dan People say that self-knowledge is the greatest virtue, but they always assume that when you do make a thorough search of yourself, you're bound to come up with something interesting: great wickedness, or sanctity, or talent. It takes real self-knowledge to recognize that you're just mediocre. That you don't honestly feel strongly enough to get out of your chair about anything. The question is, is it my fault? Or have I been dumped in a world where there's nothing left for an honest man to feel strongly about? Now there's a shallow question for you. Give me time, and I'll think of a suitably shallow answer.

Margaret Do you feel deeply about me?

Dan I can't answer that.

Edmund gets up and moves restlessly about the room. Dan and Margaret look up at him. Rachel is very self-contained

Edmund It's no good, Dan. We can't just sit here doing nothing.

Dan You can't, Ed. I can, perfectly easily.

Margaret (*sadly*) Wouldn't it be lovely if the lights just came on, without any warning. And then we could all just sit down and eat our Christmas dinner without any more fuss.

Dan Incidentally, is anybody at all hungry? Because I'm not.

Margaret Nor me.

Edmund No. I'm not either.

Dan That's a bit odd, isn't it. We ought to be by now. Whatever time it is. I was starving just before we sat down.

Edmund Well, there's plenty there, if we need it.

Margaret If it's eatable.

Edmund And tons of frozen stuff and tins in the kitchen.

Margaret Why not try it again?

Edmund Try what?

Margaret The turkey. We've all been sitting here, waiting for something to happen, but nothing has. Perhaps it's wearing off.

Dan (*to Edmund*) Do you fancy a taste?

Edmund Not much. Do you?

Margaret (*moving to the table*) Don't worry, my two heroes. I'm quite willing to try it for you. But if I collapse groaning again, I shall expect you to pick me up, at least.

Edmund Margaret, are you sure . . .?

Margaret Don't worry, Ed. For experimental reasons, if no other. (*With her fingers she picks a piece of breast meat from the bird*) There. A rather succulent piece of breast. (*She puts it in her mouth, chews it gingerly, and swallows it*)

Edmund Well?

Margaret Very nice.

Dan No pains.

Margaret No pains at all. I'm not hungry enough to enjoy it, but it tastes good.

Edmund Wait a minute. It took a few minutes to work.

Dan Not this long.

Margaret No. It's all right. I'm quite sure. (*She pours a glass of water, and drinks it*)

Edmund Did we dream it all then?

Margaret No. Before it happened. This time, it didn't.

Edmund What does it mean?

Dan It might possibly mean that whatever was happening isn't happening any more.

Edmund And that we can get out?

Dan Perhaps.

Edmund That's what I was thinking.

Pause, the two men irresolute

Margaret What are you waiting for? Do you want me to try all the doors and windows too?

Edmund Come on. The back door first.

Edmund and Dan exit urgently together into the kitchen. During the following section we hear them rattling and banging at the back door

Rachel, still sitting rigidly on the sofa, speaks quietly but tensely

Rachel Margaret!

Margaret What?

Rachel Come here.

Margaret (*going to her*) What's the matter? (*She sits down beside Rachel*)

Rachel It's so confusing . . . I don't know what's happening to me. At one moment I feel myself, and then . . .

Margaret What?

Rachel I can't say what it is, but it's something other . . . I feel it, in my body. Something coming.

Margaret What do you mean, something coming?

Rachel Something coming here.

Dan and Edmund enter from the kitchen

Edmund All right then, let's try upstairs.

Dan I don't think so, Edmund.

Edmund Let's try, anyway.

The two men exit upstairs together

Rachel It frightens me. I can't control it.

Margaret Listen Rachel, when you woke up, what happened?
You must have been dreaming, can't you remember?
Rachel I felt dizzy. I had to get out of there. There was no room.
Margaret No room?
Rachel Oh yes, something's happening now, Margaret. Whatever it is, it's
beginning!
Margaret I'll tell you what happened, Rachel! You sat up on this sofa,
bolt upright, and you looked terrified! What was happening to you?
What were you feeling, or seeing?
Rachel It was horrible, horrible, I couldn't stay in that room! I had to get
out!
Margaret What room? You were sitting here!

Dan and Edmund enter from the stairs door

Dan That's that then.
Edmund There's still the front door, and the windows.
Dan What's the point? Anyway, the windows are just the same, look!
Black as—whatever it is out there.
Margaret No way out.
Dan No, my darling, no way out.

Edmund rattles at the front door

Forget it, Ed. Forget it.
Edmund Oh God, there must be something we can do!
Dan Hard facts. Fact number one is that we're not going to get out of here
of our own volition.
Margaret Something's happening to Rachel. I don't know what it is.
Dan The question is, do I care any more?
Edmund Wait a minute! I've just remembered something!
Dan What?
Edmund The photos! The photos I took of the house, you remember, I
told you about them!
Dan I don't think I'm very interested in photos just now, Ed.
Edmund Don't you see, if it's something to do with the house, it may just
be possible . . . Where did I put them?
Rachel (*quietly*, *intensely*) No, don't look, leave them alone!
Edmund Two sets we took, as it was before we started, and as it is now . . .
Margaret Photos of the house . . . ?
Edmund You see, I just wonder . . . ?
Dan What?
Edmund Let's wait and see. Darling, where the hell are they!
Rachel It's coming nearer. I can feel it. It's almost here.
Edmund (*going to the wall units*) These drawers, Dan, help me. They're in
two separate folders.

*With desperate urgency, Edmund begins to search through the drawers. Dan
helps him, though less keenly. Margaret is still sitting next to Rachel, who is
bolt upright on the sofa, straining with intensity, almost as though listening*

Margaret (*urgently*) What is it, Rachel? What's coming nearer? What can you feel?

Rachel I don't know. I can't explain it. It's in my stomach.

Margaret Tell me! Try to tell me!

Edmund finds the folders of photographs

Edmund Here they are. Two packets of prints, before and after.

Edmund and Dan take the photographs nearer to the light of one of the candles

Margaret What is it that's coming? Where is it coming from?

Rachel Yes! It's here! Here in the house!

Margaret What?

Edmund (*looking at the photographs*) Those are the before ones. You see, that's how it was, the nettles, and the thatch all rotted and overgrown.

Dan And are those photos the ones you took, just as you took them? Do you recognize them?

Rachel The choice has been made, and now it's beginning to work.

Margaret What choice? What has been chosen?

Slowly Rachel stands up

Rachel Us. The four of us. We have been chosen.

Edmund But . . . Oh my God. Look at this one, and this. These should be the modernized pictures.

Dan They're not.

Edmund No . . . Dan, I didn't take these pictures, I've never seen the cottage like this, never, even the landscape looks different. The trees are in different places!

Dan It's almost as if . . . But it can't be, that isn't possible . . .

Edmund And this one, the long shot from the hill, look at that large house in the background, about a mile and a half from the cottage!

Dan That's the Hall! Same as in the print you gave us. I thought you said . . . ?

Edmund It was pulled down in nineteen twenty-one.

Rachel (*sweating, in anguish*) Oh God no, I don't want to, I don't want to!

Margaret What, Rachel?

Dan That one, look, that one there! That's the cottage, isn't it!

Edmund Yes, but different . . .

Dan There's someone at the window. Look. It's quite plain.

Edmund It's a woman. A dark-haired woman, with a shawl.

Rachel Yes. A dark-haired woman, with a thin face and a shawl. It's beginning.

Dan (*looking up*) How does she know?

Rachel gets up, and begins to walk slowly about the room, as she did earlier, touching, measuring, feeling. Unlike the earlier time, she seems very concentrated, and the effect is eerie. The others watch in awe-struck silence

Edmund Rachel?

Dan She's doing it again.
Margaret Don't say anything. Just watch.

Rachel begins to speak. She speaks quietly and intensely, in another character though in her own voice, without accent. In the first section she moves about the room in a kind of concentrated dream. Although the details she describes are prosaic, the voice that comes from her is strained and desperate

Rachel First I must describe my situation. The cottage is more than a hundred years old, and needs repairing. When the rain is very heavy, or goes on for a long time, the thatch leaks, or becomes soggy, and everything is damp for days. The walls are lath and plaster, and badly decayed. The plaster has crumbled in some places, and you can see daylight through the slats. I try to cover those places with sacking, as I do the windows. There has been no glass in them for as long as I can remember.
Edmund Where does she mean?
Dan Here, surely.
Edmund How can she mean here?
Margaret Be quiet.

During the next section Rachel moves towards the centre of the stage. The others watch awe-struck

Rachel (*with a deathly haunted stillness*) My own position is desperate. I try to keep my mind clear, as far as I can in my fevered condition, but the pain in my stomach is mostly very bad, and sometimes reduces me to screaming and groans, when I can do nothing but despair. For myself, I suppose I could bear it more easily, but when the children cry out and moan, and beg me for food, I feel I will run mad with anger and bitterness. It brings murder into my heart, and if I could, and it would help them, I would willingly do it. But what can I do now? Nothing. I can do nothing at all. (*Her speech dissolves into a moan of anguish and pain. For a few seconds she is reduced almost to the bellow of a wounded animal, an unearthly sound to issue from such a woman. She sinks gradually down till she is half-sitting, half-lying, supporting herself on her hands, in anguish*)
Edmund Dear God, she's in such pain!
Margaret There's nothing we can do. Just watch.
Rachel (*half-sobbing back into speech*) Oh no, there's nothing more to be done now, nothing more now. Just the waiting and the pain. The children have cried themselves to sleep, and we are all too weak to move any more. I can only sit here, talking to the walls, and wondering how long it will be.
Edmund What is she saying?
Dan What children?
Margaret Just listen. Go on, Rachel, we can all hear.
Rachel If I could write, I would put it all down in a book, so that the whole world should know what they've done to us. But no-one bothers to teach the poor, so even that comfort is denied me. But I have to speak. I have to make it known, even if only to the bare walls!
Edmund Who is it? Who is it speaking?

Margaret I don't know. Just listen.

Rachel I, Sarah Jane Malby, born a Christian, aged twenty-six years, a married woman, but now a widow, am lying here on a straw mattress with my two children, Robert and Jane. There is a little water, but nothing to eat. We have none of us eaten for well over a week at least. I don't remember when.

Edmund Here. In this house.

Margaret Listen.

Rachel My husband Robert was a hard-working man, not sparing himself when there was farm work or anything else to be had, and we were all happy till the bad times came. The people had to leave for the town, and many houses in the village stood empty. There was no trade and no work, till bread became too dear to buy, and then there was none at all to be had. The Squire told us there was no more work, and we must fend for ourselves, and the Parson told us to pray to God. We did pray. We prayed to him day and night. But the food got less and less, and my husband was in despair. He took to going out at night, and some nights he'd bring back a rabbit or a hen, even a lamb one time, and we managed to live for several months that way. But the gamekeepers got stricter, a man in the next village was hanged, and there was no more game to be had, with half the country living on it. A man came one night, a stranger with a book in his hand, and he talked to Robert till dawn. They spoke angrily, and cried out, so that I heard it, and the children stirred in their sleep. Then, the next night, Robert went out with that man and some others, and he didn't come back the next morning. And I heard that there were fires in the fields, the ricks were burning, and the Squire's barn had been burned down, and that my Robert had been taken by the soldiers.

Edmund Rachel, darling . . .!

Margaret No, you must let her finish.

Rachel is still half-seated, half-leaning centre stage, with the others watching her. Her stillness, and the intensity of what she is saying, rivets everyone to the spot

Rachel I went to the Assizes. I saw my Robert in the dock with the other men, looking pale and ill. I was praying for transportation, but it was death. I cried out to the judge that we were all starving, and what were we expected to do without food. But the judge spoke grandly about property and rights, and I was dragged from the court. I took the two children to see their father hanged. I told them to remember what was being done to him, so that they should grow up to avenge his death on all the wicked men responsible. But that will never happen now. A doctor told me it takes twenty minutes for a hanging man to die. I stood there all the time, without taking my eyes off his poor face, giving him all my love to help him bear that terrible death. He moved a little at first, but gradually became still. But I waited over half an hour, to be quite sure. None of us cried. Not even the children.

Edmund Barbarians, barbarians!

Rachel gets up and moves about as though re-living the experience

Rachel That evening I tried to see the Squire. But they chased me away, and said my husband was a criminal. I crept round the side of the house, hoping to go in and tell the Squire of my children's hunger, and ask for his mercy. When I got to the window, I could see them at table. The Squire was there, and his brother the Parson, and his sons. There was a side of beef, and several roast chicken, and cakes, and pies, and bottles of red wine.

The sound of the harpsichord melody is plainly though faintly heard. They all hear it, and instinctively look at the instrument in the corner, which remains quite still

And in the corner, the Squire's daughter was playing music, a sweet melancholy tune, while my husband lay dead, and my children were crying for food. And I thought, this can never be forgiven, no circumstance, no degree of self-interest, not even ignorance can ever excuse this feasting and dancing, while on the same planet, in the same village, people are starving. And I knew then that I was beaten, that where there was no conscience, there was no hope, that there was nothing to be done, that this wickedness and injustice was too great a monster for me to grapple with. I came home, and closed the door, and since that day no-one has bothered to open it to see who may be inside. (*She reaches the sofa and sinks down on it, sitting rigid and still*)

The music imperceptibly fades away

Edmund (*horrified*) Here she means. She means here.

Rachel I used to believe in God. But this world is men's work, I recognize it by the bloodstains. If God still sees us, he sees us with despair. Like Pilate, he shakes his head, and washes his hands, unable to save us. I know we will soon be dead now. The worst pain is over, and my bodily weakness is almost comforting, like the beginning of sleep. I have no forgiveness for the selfishness and greed which has destroyed my family. The hardest thing of my dying is to know that our murderers will go unpunished. Someone, surely, must pay for our unjust deaths—and all the other deaths like ours, for I know we are not unique. If no ear can hear my accusations, nor no eye ever read them, let my words burn themselves into the fabric of these walls, so that brickwork and plaster and beams should remember the agony and injustice of those dying under this roof. How can this ground ever be easy, while there is no atonement for crimes like these. The soil is bitter with my children's blood . . . I can't say any more, just this cry against injustice, from the dark centuries. Jane is dead now, I think, and Robert is in a deep sleep from which he will never wake. I can't speak any more. I shall need all my breath to face this starvation that is slowly draining my life . . . While we sleep in our paupers' graves, let someone, somewhere, remember . . . (*Her eyes close, and she falls silent, rigid, and swaying slightly*)

No-one moves

Margaret Us. The chosen four.

Rachel slowly topples on to the sofa, and from there to the floor, where she lies quite still. This breaks the mood, and the others rush to her

Edmund Rachel!
Dan Is she all right?
Edmund She's dead!
Margaret No she isn't. She's still breathing. Rachel ...? Rachel ...? She's coming round.

Slowly Rachel sits up, looking dazed

Edmund Rachel, my darling, are you all right?

Rachel doesn't answer, but looks round at the room

Rachel We must put out all the candles.

The others are mystified at her quietness and certainty, the more so when she begins to stand up

Dan Put out the candles? Why?
Rachel Put out all the candles, and go upstairs.
Margaret (*quietly*) Why go upstairs Rachel?
Rachel Because she's there. Lying on a straw mattress with her two children. Where our bed used to be. Under the cracked walls and the leaking roof, with mice running between her feet. The children are stiff and still, with their fragile bones protruding, and their skin like paper. She's half-sitting up against the wall. She wouldn't die on her back. Her eyes are open, and the expression on her face—is not an expression of peace ... Follow me. (*She moves slowly towards the stairs*)

The candles are now all extinguished except one, and the stage is lit by the illumination from that one only, and the dying fire

Edmund Shall we go? (*He follows Rachel*)
Dan I don't think we have any choice.

Rachel exits, followed by Edmund

Margaret has the last candle, and she and Dan go to the stairs door

Margaret Hold my hand, Dan. I'm frightened.
Dan Don't be afraid. I told you we were privileged.
Margaret Yes. And I understand it now. Now I understand it. (*She blows out the last candle*)

Dan and Margaret exit through the stairs door together

For a few moments the stage remains in darkness apart from a faint glow from the fire. Then, gradually, electric lights begin to come on, the television clicks on to a frame scan, red lights come on at the radio and stereo, the Christmas tree lights come on, a blaze of light shines in from the kitchen and there is a busy, efficient humming of electrical equipment. It is as though the set has come to life. From the radio comes the faint sound of light, anonymous music. Suddenly, when the stage is fully illuminated, and all the equipment working, the television frame scan clicks into the middle of a BBC newscast

Newsreader (*from the TV*) The Minister of Transport has ordered an enquiry into yesterday's motorway pile-up, in which more than two hundred vehicles are thought to have been involved. No casualty figures are yet available, but they are thought to be certain to push the holiday accident toll to a new record level ... The Chairman of the World Famine Relief Organization, speaking at a UNESCO conference in Paris on Europe and the under-developed world, has called for a radical heart-searching on the part of the developed countries. It is well known, he said, that under the present circumstances, far from rectifying the situation the rich countries are getting richer, and the poor countries are getting poorer. How much longer are we prepared to let this situation continue, he asked the assembled delegates. His question was received in silence ... Finally, news is just coming in of a bizarre Christmas tragedy. In a remote country cottage, four apparently healthy people in their late thirties have been found dead. An air of mystery surrounds the story at the moment, said a spokesman at Scotland Yard, but foul play is not suspected. The four bodies, when found, were in an extremely emaciated condition, and although the house was full of food and drink, and a sumptuous Christmas dinner was laid on the table, almost untouched, all four people appear to have died of starvation.

The newscast clicks off into the frame scan again. Slowly, and in a silence broken only by the humming of the electrical equipment, the CURTAIN *falls on the brightly illuminated stage*

FURNITURE AND PROPERTY LIST

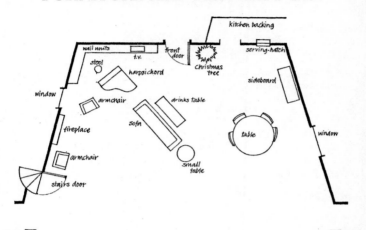

ACT I

On stage:
Sofa
Armchairs
Inglenook fireplace
Coffee table
Small table (by sofa) *On it:* table lamp (practical)
Drinks table. *On it:* glasses, bottles of drink including sherry, brandy, *Campari*, soda syphon, jug of water, ice bucket containing ice cubes
Wall units. *On shelves:* books, records, stereo equipment, TV (practical), telephone. *In drawers:* two folders of photographs
Christmas tree (decorated) *Under it:* wrapped presents (including a framed print for **Rachel**)
Harpsichord (or clavichord)
Stool (by harpsichord)
Shelves. *On them:* music scores
Dining table. *On it:* tablecloth, 4 plates, 4 knives, 4 forks, 4 spoons, 4 wine glasses, 4 water glasses, jug of water, cruet, carving-knife and fork, 2 candles in holders, box of matches, corkscrew, serving-spoons
Sideboard
Carpet
Window curtains
On walls: pictures and prints, clock, spotlights (practical)
Free-standing spotlights (practical)

Off stage: Bag. *In it:* wrapped box containing small African carving of woman
                 giving birth; bottle of smelling salts **(Dan)**
                 Bottle of burgundy wine **(Dan)**
                 Turkey on carving dish **(Edmund)**
                 Dish of roast potatoes **(Rachel)**
                 Dish of brussels sprouts **(Rachel)**
                 Bread sauce **(Margaret)**
                 Cranberry jelly **(Margaret)**
                 4 Victorian candlesticks with candles **(Edmund** and **Dan)**
                 Cloth **(Rachel)**
                 Torch **(Edmund)**
                 Hammer **(Edmund)**

Personal: **Edmund:** wristwatch
                 Rachel: wristwatch
                 Dan: wristwatch
                 Margaret: wristwatch

ACT II

Off stage: Pile of blankets **(Margaret)**

Personal: **Margaret:** handkerchief

LIGHTING PLOT

Practical fittings required: free-standing and wall-mounted spotlights (one angled to shine on centre of dining table); table lamp, Christmas tree lights, fire effect, television

Interior. A cottage. The same scene throughout

ACT I.   Afternoon

To open: Darkness

Cue 1	When ready *Slowly build up effect of winter afternoon light, fire effect,* *Christmas tree lights, artificial light from kitchen*	(Page 1)
Cue 2	**Rachel:** ". . . I think that's right . . ." *Begin very slow fade as dusk falls*	(Page 9)
Cue 3	**Edmund** switches on table lamp and spotlights *Snap on table lamp and spotlights*	(Page 11)
Cue 4	**Edmund** switches on spotlight angled at dining table *Snap on spotlight angled to shine on dining table*	(Page 14)
Cue 5	**Edmund:** "Not too badly . . ." *Black-out, including property fittings, but leaving fire effect*	(Page 15)
Cue 6	As **Edmund** and **Dan** place lighted candles around room *Bring up effect of candlelight—dim shadowy light*	(Page 18)
Cue 7	**Edmund:** "We can't get out." *Black-out*	(Page 27)

ACT II

To open: As at end of ACT I before Black-out (*Cue* 7)

Cue 8	As candles are extinguished *Fade lighting, leaving fire effect*	(Page 57)
Cue 9	When ready *Gradually snap on all practicals, including TV on frame scan*	(Page 57)
Cue 10	When stage is fully illuminated *Snap on TV newscast effect*	(Page 58)
Cue 11	**Newsreader:** ". . . died of starvation." *Snap on TV frame scan*	(Page 58)

EFFECTS PLOT

ACT I

Cue 1   As CURTAIN rises   (Page 1)
Faint harpsichord music—fade as Lights come up

Cue 2   When ready   (Page 1)
Footsteps from above, then descending stairs

Cue 3   **Dan, Margaret** and **Edmund** stop groaning   (Page 21)
Very faint harpsichord music—increase slightly as they get up from the floor

Cue 4   **Margaret:** "Was it like that with you?"   (Page 22)
Fade harpsichord music

Cue 5   **Edmund** exits into kitchen   (Page 26)
Sound of door being rattled, off L

ACT II

Cue 6   As CURTAIN rises   (Page 28)
Intermittent banging from above

Cue 7   **Margaret:** ". . . for five minutes, please."   (Page 28)
Stop banging

Cue 8   **Rachel:** ". . . A long way off."   (Page 30)
Pause, then start distant rumbling, gradually increasing volume until very loud

Cue 9   **Margaret:** "It's bursting my eardrums . . .!"   (Page 30)
Increase rumbling to unendurable level for a few seconds, then stop suddenly; then sound of breaking glass as window falls in

Cue 10   **Edmund:** ". . . know where to look."   (Page 45)
Footsteps descending stairs

Cue 11   **Edmund** and **Dan** exit into kitchen   (Page 51)
Sound of door being rattled, off L

Cue 12   **Rachel:** ". . . bottles of red wine."   (Page 56)
Faint but clear harpsichord music

Cue 13   **Rachel:** ". . . who may be inside."   (Page 56)
Fade harpsichord music

Cue 14   As practicals come on   (Page 57)
Build up humming of electrical equipment and faint, light, anonymous music from radio

Cue 15   When stage is fully illuminated   (Page 58)
Snap on TV newscast